SMALL PERIOD

GARDENS

SMALL PERIOD
GARDENS

A PRACTICAL GUIDE TO DESIGN AND PLANTING

ROY STRONG

HISTORICAL PLANT LISTS COMPILED BY TONY LORD

RIZZOLI
NEW YORK

This book is a response to the huge renaissance in garden history of the last twenty years. Few of those books deal with the practical realities of period gardens, particularly small ones. As a result garden history has tended to remain on the bookshelf. But it shouldn't, for there is so much to learn, copy and adapt from the garden styles of the past. This portfolio of designs, or evocations as I would prefer to call them, attempts to open up all sorts of exciting possibilities for today's gardeners.

The project has been a demanding one, asking for expertise over a wide range of subjects and periods. For checking all the planting and for compiling the plant list I am more than grateful to Tony Lord. For the elegant design which lucidly presents complex material I am grateful to Prue Bucknall, and to Gill Tomblin I owe a debt once more for visualizing the historic reference material and designs as I saw them in my mind's eye.

ROY STRONG

PAGE 1 A wall fountain, based on one designed by Sir Edwin Lutyens in the early twentieth century, making typical use of verncacular materials, stone and tile, to frame a sculpted lion's mask against a rendered wall.

PAGE 2 A box and gravel parterre at West Green House, Hampshire, planted in the early years of this century in the heyday of the revival of formality and supposedly based on seventeenth-century patterns. It was elaborated in the 1970s by the addition of topiary cones and standards.

PAGE 3 The back garden of a town house in Bristol, c.1800. The door which leads out to the road beyond is camouflaged with an elegant treillage gazebo.

First published in the United States of America in 1992
by Rizzoli International Publications, Inc.
300 Park Avenue South, New York, NY 10010

First published in Great Britain in 1992 by Conran Octopus Limited

Library of Congress Cataloging-in-Publication Data
Strong, Roy C
Small period gardens: a practical guide to design and planting
Roy Strong: historical plant lists compiled by Tony Lord.
p. cm.
Includes bibliographical references and index.
ISBN 0–8478–1551–X
1. Gardens—Design. 2. Historic gardens. I. Lord, Tony.
II. Title.
SB473.S848 1992
712'. 6—dc20 91–51010 CIP

Illustrator Gill Tomblin
Plant Consultant Tony Lord
Designer Prue Bucknall
Picture Research Nadine Bazar
Production Alison McIver

DTP Ruth Prentice, Alison Shackleton
Printed in Hong Kong

CONTENTS

Inspiration from the Past

RIGHT The recently planted box and gravel parterre in my garden was inspired by those in the re-created garden of William III at Het Loo in the Netherlands, which was originally designed in the 1680s. Although only 15 ft (4.6 m) square, it retains the essence of the original, a huge swirling pattern of green turf, box hedging, statuary and coloured gravels.

The monogram in the middle will eventually form the initials of my wife and myself, an idea which goes back to the first century AD, and which adds a delightfully personal and commemorative touch to a garden.

RIGHT Arabella Lennox Boyd successfully distilled the elements of a pre-1914 country house garden in the grand manner into a tiny area for the Chelsea Flower Show in 1990. She combined a strong evergreen structure in yew and box with a soft, luxurious planting – a haze of silvery-grey and mauve. The plants included *Onopordum acanthium*, digitalis, a cardoon, *Allium aflatunense* and several grey-leaved artemisias. A similar plan would make a beautiful small town garden, looked over from a terrace or balcony, although I would have preferred a statue or small fountain as a central focal point, to introduce a different texture and year-round interest.

*E*very time we walk in a garden, even if it has only just been planted, we walk through history. A simple wooden pergola garlanded with fragrant climbers is not simply a reminder of the legacy of Miss Jekyll and the country house gardens of Edwardian England, but the latest in a long and noble line of descent reaching back via the gardens of Renaissance Italy to those which the ancient Romans planted round their villas. Pliny the Younger, who drew such a vivid picture of the delights of Roman villa gardens, would feel quite at ease with such a structure, although the planting would surprise him, for the repertory of climbers has been infinitely enriched over the centuries. An island bed planted with evergreens and flowering shrubs behind a foreground of perennials and annuals also has a long ancestry, going back to the eighteenth-century delight in sinuous serpentine lines and enthusiasm for the new plants then arriving from America, South Africa and Australia. Even a simple paved terrace with one or two steps down is also a response to history, owing its

Two views of the decorator John Fowler's garden at King John's Hunting Lodge, Odiham, Hampshire, which although planted after 1945 nevertheless kept alive the pre-1914 formal tradition of England. Fowler adapted many of the elements of that style and showed how successfully they could articulate a relatively small space. Fowler worked with the American decorator Nancy Lancaster, and it is difficult to believe that in its use of box-edged beds and simple topiary (left) this section of the garden was not influenced by the re-creations of the historic gardens of colonial Williamsburg (see pages 58-61).

The planting, however, remains within the cottage garden tradition of Gertrude Jekyll. The view above betrays Fowler's keen appreciation of seventeenth-century garden design. Here an eighteenth-century figure of a shepherd frames a vista leading to a garden gate, along a gravel path which is flanked by hornbeam hedges and clipped box in tubs. In winter the hedge changes colour to russet.

9

The garden at 100 Cheyne Walk, Chelsea, London, was laid out by Sir Edwin Lutyens before 1913 and reworked in the late 1980s by Arabella Lennox Boyd. Originally the central turf panel had a circular lily pond and the flanking paths culminated in niches containing classical statues. Essentially Lutyens was creating, in terms of his own time, a seventeenth-century turf parterre.

origins to the revolutionary method of articulating space by means of hard structure initiated by the architect Bramante in the sixteenth century. In fact every part of any garden is an expression of a part of this history, including the plants. Some, such as rosemary, would have been familiar to medieval gardeners, who would have planted it in pots and turned it into topiary. Others, such as pelargoniums and begonias, first entered the garden in the Victorian age, heralding the great era of 'bedding out'.

It is an astonishingly rich heritage, and it is equally surprising how slow we have been to appreciate it, let alone make use of it. It is this more than anything else that has prompted me to write this book, an attempt to open up the treasure trove of past centuries to a much wider audience. And certainly its aim is not only an armchair appreciation of the possibilities offered, but also a practical one, for the past is full of superb ideas for even the tiniest of today's gardens. These range from different ways of actually looking at and thinking about gardens, which are both liberating and refreshing, to the rediscovery of forgotten elements

LEFT A small American front garden in Seattle which was designed in 1988, yet whose origins go back to the quartered box-edged geometric gardens of the Renaissance. On any scale this formula remains a timeless classic, used again and again over the centuries. A vase provides an unpretentious focal point, at the same time as giving much needed height.

BELOW A garden designed in the late 1960s by, surprisingly, the modernist Thomas Church (1902-78) in San Francisco, California. Although he was an apostle of the new and one of the few designers of private gardens in a contemporary idiom, as opposed to a nostalgic one, Church could equally well plunder the dressing-up box of the past when he thought it appropriate. In this garden box-edged beds with an almost rococo rhythm to them provide a handsome framework for a vivid display of roses.

An English garden at Rofford Manor, Oxfordshire, designed in the 1980s by Michael Balston from an amalgam of elements which constitute what is now recognized internationally as the classic turn-of-the-century country house style. The soft foreground planting in pinks, greys and mauves is pure Gertrude Jekyll, as is the lush planting which breaks the line of the hard structure. All of the structural elements seen here are available today in reproduction.

which can still be used in making them, such as turf parterres, or estrade trees.

The history of gardens, as viewed from today's standpoint, is inevitably the history of large gardens. There are two main reasons for this. Firstly, small gardens from the past have simply not survived, and secondly, those that did exist have only rarely left any visual records. The scarcity of such material relating to small gardens before the last century should be borne in mind by anyone using this book. It is also easy to forget that the small garden as we know it today was essentially a nineteenth-century invention. Before then the pleasure garden was the prerogative of royalty, the aristocracy and the gentry. The most anyone below that rank could aspire to was the cultivation of produce to eke out a meagre diet. We, of course, live in a very different kind of society which can afford to indulge in design options which would have been open only to a privileged few in previous ages. And why not? We also enjoy another huge advantage: we can bring to earlier styles the labour-saving devices of the late twentieth century.

This approach has certainly affected the planning and design of my own garden over the last twenty years. The avenues and axes were inspired by bird's-eye views of late seventeenth-century formal gardens, from which I learned about the importance of vistas and perspective in design, and the art of achieving through them drama, surprise and optical illusion. The steps, balustrading and statuary reflect many visits to the great Renaissance and baroque gardens of Italy, where such elements were originally a startling novelty. They taught me how even the most modest amount of built hard structure in a garden will give year-round interest and provide vertical accents, pattern and focal points to hold the composition together. As the garden has developed more has been added in response to particular encounters with the past. A parterre of swirling curves in evergreen box set against coloured gravels, with a monogram of the initials of my wife and myself at the centre, was inspired by visits to the great restored garden of the 1680s at Het Loo in the Netherlands. There the equivalent was more than a hundred feet (30 metres) square, but we managed to distil its

The rose garden at Mottisfont Priory, Romsey, Hampshire, was laid out in 1972-3, and added to in 1985-7, to house the National Trust's collection of old and rare roses. Part of the inspiration for its design was Victorian, from an age when the rose garden first emerged as a garden feature, prompting the invention of all kinds of support structures to display the delicate blooms. Here the vista leads to a glorious circular arcade festooned with *Rosa* 'Débutante' and *R.* 'Bleu Magenta'.

RIGHT This patio garden in the Palacia de Viana, Seville, Spain, is one of sixteen small garden enclosures, each focusing on a cooling fountain. Here we see a different garden tradition, the Islamic one, assimilated into the Western tradition and proving admirably suited to the Spanish climate. The edging of the beds with brilliant blue ceramic tiles is typical of Spanish and Portuguese gardens. Although the palace dates back to the sixteenth century, the asymmetrical layout is unlikely to be earlier than the late nineteenth century.

ABOVE Created in about 1970, this tiny contemporary box parterre in the garden of the late Roderick Cameron at Saint-Jean-Cap-Ferrat, Alpes-Maritimes, France, was inspired by Italian Renaissance prototypes which can still be seen today (see page 25). The formula is very simple: two hedges of clipped box, one inside the other, contain ground-cover planting, a classic terracotta container providing a strong vertical focal point to each half of the divided rectangle.

essence into a space about fifteen feet (4.5 metres) square. Elsewhere an Italian baroque statue of spring presides happily over two tiny Jacobean knot gardens, and topiary peacocks, derived from the gardens of the Arts and Crafts movement from the turn of the century, stand sentry at the entrance to another part of the garden.

This mélange may give the reader an idea of how the dressing-up box of the past can be rummaged through for ideas for today. None of the historic design features in my own garden is an exact re-creation, but rather they make use of elements from the past translated into terms of today's gardens, bearing in mind the commitment involved in the way of time and labour. Wholesale period re-creation is another option, and has provided the structure of this book, for it is intended, too, for gardeners who wish to experiment with styles and techniques from history in order to complement the style of a particular house. This may mean adding a garden where there would never have been one originally, but why not plant a Tudor knot behind a half-timbered sixteenth-century cottage, or design a garden based on

a Renaissance pergola to complement a converted farmhouse in Tuscany?

And this brings me to the notion of 're-creation'. I have described the garden designs in this book as 'evocations' for specific reasons. Having been trained as an historian, I am acutely aware that there is no such thing as an archaeologically exact re-creation of a garden style from the past. There can only be approximations, ranging from the fairly exact to the wildly inaccurate. Although in this book every effort has been made within each period to provide an authentic garden type, together with its correct planting and backed up by documentary visual evidence, compromise of some kind remains inevitable. Running a plastic edging to mark out the curves of a baroque parterre is the application of a practical modern solution to an age-old problem. And if Le Nôtre were around today he would bless its invention. The use of modern, more disease-resistant and repeat-flowering roses which nevertheless preserve the colour and fragrance of the nineteenth-century originals makes equally good sense when planning a Victorian rose garden. Again, if William Paul could return today that is surely precisely what he would do. And a wild planting of spring flowers unknown in medieval times will give the effect of the flowery meads we see in illuminated manuscripts, but without all the attendant maintenance problems.

This book is aimed to be liberating and not constraining, asking the user to mix, match and adapt whatever he or she wants from it. There is no reason why you should not take the Italian Renaissance pergola structure, for example, and clothe it with climbers no one would have known at the time. The result would not be a model of period exactitude, but it would be a none the less valid and happy use of the inspiration of the past. Some of the old garden forms also ask only to be revived and re-invented for today's gardens. The turf garden or *parterre à l'angloise*, for instance, a pattern of turf set against coloured gravels, could be used to make extraordinarily exciting gardens, employing decorative designs later than those of the baroque era. And surely there is someone who could design a twentieth-century knot? So do not be inhibited by the past; rather let it work for you.

Plundering the past is by no means a new idea for gardeners. Both the Renaissance garden and the eighteenth-century English landscape garden were attempts to re-create the villa garden of classical antiquity, for instance, while in the nineteenth century gardens were planted in the Elizabethan, baroque, rococo and Italian Renaissance styles – albeit with stolidly Victorian results. It is only in our own century, however, that we have become self-conscious about looking backwards, as new ideas have come into play. The notion of preserving historic gardens for their own sake arose largely as a result of the two world wars and the ensuing social revolutions, which saw palace and country house gardens passing into the hands of the public, and has given rise to a serious discipline of historic garden conservation and restoration. The question of where garden restoration ends and re-creation begins is beyond the scope of this book, but it is an important point to bear in mind. Such problems do not arise, of course, where it has been decided to add a period garden to an historic building which had none before. More complex issues arise in the case of gardens which are re-creations of those which once stood on site, but it still remains a great leap from this to putting a garden back, particularly when, as is the case with most small gardens,

FAR LEFT, ABOVE The structure of this late seventeenth-century *plate-bande* in contemporary guise, at Little Haseley, in Oxfordshire, remains traditional: a narrow border edged with clipped box with vertical accents (here modern standard roses) at regular intervals. A mixed herbaceous planting has replaced the staggered, symmetrical exhibition of flowers which would have filled such a border three centuries earlier.

LEFT ABOVE A narrow pergola in the garden of the designer David Hicks, created in the 1980s, from inexpensive larch poles, is an elegant reinterpretation of the classic rustic rose pergola, favoured by the Arts and Crafts Movement of the late nineteenth century, but whose antecedents go back as far as the tunnel arbours of the Middle Ages.

FAR LEFT, BELOW George London and Henry Wise described how to achieve this effect in *The Retir'd Gard'ner* (1706), using an elm grown to 6 ft (1.83 m) in height, with its head clipped into a ball, and forming its 'container' out of hornbeam (*Carpinus betulus*). Here the idea is updated in a garden of the 1980s, using a standard euonymus underplanted with origanum in a 'tub' of box. There are many possible variants of this effect on a small scale: a standard crataegus could rise from a 'tub' of purple berberis, or an *Amelanchier lamarckii* could emerge from a 'pot' of green box or crataegus.

LEFT BELOW Another superb modern instance of training in the seventeenth-century manner is to be found in this small spring parterre, created in the 1980s at Stavordale Priory, Somerset. It is presided over by standard forsythias, which after a few weeks of stunning spring glory tend sadly to be rather dull. The enclosing border is a modern version of the *plate-bande*, but using Irish yew (*Taxus baccata* 'Fastigiata'), unknown before 1780, in place of the usual clipped yew (*Taxus baccata*) or juniper. The planting in between is in the abundant late Victorian manner.

OPPOSITE The herbaceous borders at the House of Pitmuies, Forfar, Scotland, were originally cut between the wars and are a magical reminder of a long and popular tradition. Borders such as these were planted at Arley Hall, Cheshire, as early as the 1840s and went into eclipse during the heyday of bedding out in mid-Victorian times, only to return to favour at the end of the century under the aegis of William Robinson and Gertrude Jekyll. The border of 'old-fashioned' perennials and annuals has never lost its appeal as a classic garden feature and is still attempted by gardeners today around the world, even in the more unfavourable climes.

LEFT Avenues were the invention of the Renaissance, when the rules of scientific perspective began to be applied to garden design. In the centuries that followed, the approach to the villa or great house was always by way of an avenue of cypresses, oaks, limes or chestnuts. But the same sort of effect can also be achieved today on a very modest scale and with only minimum maintenance. Here, at Westwell Manor, Oxfordshire, is a recently planted avenue of *Malus* 'John Downie', a small tree which bears wonderfully profuse blossom in spring and glorious fruits in autumn. The path is of the simplest, just a mown way through long grass. Alternative trees would be standard maples, *Quercus ilex, Robinia pseudoacacia* 'Inermis', *Amerlanchier lamarckii* or beech. Some of these would require annual clipping and pruning. In the flower garden standard roses can be planted as an avenue, and standard gooseberries can serve the same function in the potager.

there are no visual records of the original appearance. And allowances also have to be made for the availability or otherwise of period plants, and even more for maintenance problems. Most period gardens, large or small, were made in an age when labour was cheap. Today it is not, and any re-creation will inevitably be tempered by that consideration. None of this need deter anyone wishing to create a small period garden, who should be aware of these facts but not inhibited by them. For an increased knowledge of garden history not only enriches visits to historic gardens, but also adds greatly to the pleasure to be derived from one's own.

Every garden down the ages has been created for delight, and for the enjoyment of all of the senses. More importantly – though it is something we have tended to forget – they also engaged the intellect and the mind. In this century we have impoverished the idea of the garden in many ways. The perfect voyage into the past, involving as it does the rediscovery of lost skills and experiences, should not be sterile and escapist, but move us forward creatively – and that is what I hope this book will do.

Ages of Adventure

1420~1620

Gardening is a mirror of history. It is a product of peace and security, an affirmation of faith in the future, practised by man in the confident knowledge that he may sit in his old age in the shadow of the vine he has planted. It is also an expression of delight in the joys of this life – however much it was glossed over in medieval times as an anticipation of the paradise to come in the next. When the millennium passed and the world did not come to its feared apocalyptic end, a new expectancy began to quicken about this life, one in which gardening was gradually to find a place. And by gardening I mean the horticultural

In this small late medieval garden depicted in a French manuscript, *Livre du Coeur d'Amours espris,* of about 1465, a tunnel arbour of trellis covered with vines abuts the castle walls, while a Gothic door and windows made in the tunnel give on to a small grass enclosure, or herber. A trellis fence covered in double roses shields the garden on one side, and in the corners of the turf benches which run around the edges are two small fruit trees.

The tunnel arbour remained a classic
garden feature for over three hundred
years, until the close of the seventeenth
century. It was designed to provide
outdoor walks sheltered from the sun. This
one, at Winchester, Hampshire, is part of
a re-creation dating from 1986 of a late
thirteenth-century garden such as Edward
I's queen, Eleanor of Castile, might have
known. Like the tunnel arbour shown on
pages 20-21, it also abuts a wall and
supports a vine. Tunnel arbours were also
a typical feature of Italian Renaissance
gardens as well as those of the Northern
Renaissance; and were the forerunners of
today's pergolas.

The medieval garden at The Cloisters, New York, is a combination of elements from late medieval sources, such as brick-edged raised beds and wattle fencing, but was never intended to be an archaeologically correct re-creation of a medieval garden. When it was laid out in the 1930s it was a pioneering project; since that time our knowledge of medieval gardens has increased considerably.

arts as a whole, practised not just for the sake of plants' edible fruits or healing properties, but also purely to give pleasure. In the West, this sort of gardening only narrowly survived the Dark Ages, through the monastic tradition of cultivating flowers with which to decorate altar and church on festival days. Late medieval secular gardens owed their development more to Islamic horticulture, through which they spread north from Spain into France, Italy, England and Germany in the thirteenth century. Gardening for pleasure in the West in the Middle Ages was the prerogative of an élite ruling class, an expression of an increasingly elaborate culture in which leisure and an appreciation of cultivated nature played an important part. It was to retain that element of exclusiveness up until the nineteenth century, which saw the birth of what we recognize today as the small garden.

The medieval and Renaissance periods embrace over five centuries of garden-making, from about the year 1000 to the first quarter of the seventeenth century. Even in a thumbnail sketch, such a great stretch of time needs to be broken down into three distinct phases: the medieval period, about 1000 to 1500; the garden revolution initiated by the Italian Renaissance, from about 1450 to 1600; and the impact of this on countries north of the Alps, from about 1500 to 1620. Each of these phases produced quite distinct and recognizable styles, some of which we can still experience in surviving gardens, albeit changed, but most of which we can relive only through contemporary pictorial evidence. Inevitably the story is that of great gardens, for any garden-making beyond the cultivation of fruit and vegetables was a privilege of the leisured class throughout this period.

But we are fortunate in that the gardens of our earliest garden style, the medieval, were by their very nature small. Although we know that the medieval garden passed through successive phases over five centuries, virtually all the visual evidence we have belongs to the fifteenth century. Most of it also comes from the Netherlands where, as a consequence of the move towards hyper-realism in painting from Van Eyck (*d.*1441) onwards, the most detailed records were made of the appearance of the gardens. As medieval Europe was a cultural unity, however, this format, with due allowance for variations

in planting in different climatic conditions, can be taken as typical. Its basic elements had already taken shape by the twelfth century. The garden was always an enclosure, often surrounded by a ditch, and contained by a hedge, a wall or a fence of wattle or lattice-work, which might have vines, roses or honeysuckle clambering over or through it. Against the containing walls or hedge would be turf benches, sometimes planted with flowers. The central area might be a flowery mead or lawn, perhaps crossed by paths, or the whole area could equally well be flagged or gravelled and have raised beds set into it. These beds would have been contained by low walls of planks or brick courses, and again filled with turf into which flowers, topiary and shrubs would be planted. Pietro de' Crescenzi, who wrote one of the few medieval manuals on gardening

(1305), records that the average size of a burgher's garden was five-eighths of an acre (about one quarter of a hectare) but a king or rich lord's was over twelve acres (4.85 hectares). By the fourteenth century gardens could be subdivided into elaborate patchworks of kitchen gardens, pond gardens and herbers for pleasure, often with enclosed woods and parkland for the chase.

With medieval gardens, therefore, re-creating the structure seems to pose few problems and to be relatively inexpensive. The problems start to arise in their planting and maintenance. It should also be remembered that the attitude to plants and gardens was very different from our own. The approach then was more complex, taking into account not only their beauty but also their usefulness and fragrance. Moreover each flower

LEFT The Villa Medici, Fiesole, Florence, Italy, was designed by Michelozzo and constructed between 1460 and 1470. Even after five hundred years this garden has retained its original structure, embodying elements of the Renaissance garden revolution: the garden looks outwards to enjoy the landscape, and the hillside has been cut into a terrace. From a vine-covered pergola we look down on geometric *compartimenti* with a fountain as a focal point. Although changed, the planting still respects the original concept, using topiary evergreens and hedging to provide vertical accents and delineate ground pattern.

RIGHT The garden of the Palazzo Piccolomini, Pienza, Italy, built by Bernardo Rossellino for Pope Pius II between 1450 and 1463, is a miraculous survival of a small Renaissance garden, laid out on axis with the rear façade of the palace. Although the garden is enclosed, the main path leads to a stunning vista over the countryside. While the planting has changed, the layout retains its symmetrical geometry of quartered beds with a fountain as a focal point.

had its own specific symbolic significance, just as the garden as a whole was interpreted as a symbol of the earthly paradise. Flowers not only adorned the garden, but were also woven into garlands and chaplets, used to decorate churches on feast days, cut for the house and given as presents. Their fragrance offset the pungent smells of the pre-plumbing age, and their healing and purgative properties were essential to the practice of medicine. The iris, for example, enjoyed all the virtues: it was strongly perfumed; it was beautiful, in shades of blue, white and yellow; its roots could be utilized to make ink or powdered and used as an air freshener; its leaves were used for thatching; it had a wide variety of medicinal uses; and in its white form it was taken to symbolize virginity.

If the medieval garden was designed to be looked down

upon by the eye of God, its Renaissance successor found its optical focus in the eye of man. That huge movement which we define as the Renaissance placed man firmly at the centre of his world, arranging and defining space around him in terms of the new and scientific art of perspective. This had a revolutionary impact on garden design, for instead of the garden being viewed in the medieval way as a series of isolated incidents, all of its ingredients were now marshalled in response to a single-point perspective, the rays of which converged in the eyes of the viewer. It was to be the greatest of all garden revolutions, for it gave rise to those elements which are still fundamental to garden-making today: vistas, avenues and cross-axes. These were used not only to divide a garden into geometric shapes on a grid system, but also to hold it together. For to a

Renaissance man number was the key to the divine harmony of the universe, which was expressed in mathematical proportion, geometry, symmetry and perspective. The medieval garden had been one of parts. The Renaissance garden, while still made up of parts, was conceived as a unity.

Renaissance man believed that to know God's world was in fact to know Him. In the garden this belief was pursued through the subtle interplay of art and nature. Sometimes nature was transformed by human skill into art, as in the development of topiary. Sometimes art was deployed in skilful imitation of nature, as in the grottoes that now became popular, constructed of stalactites, tufa and shells. Gardens in which nature had been rearranged by the hand of man into geometry were an expression of divine order. The garden with its circles

OPPOSITE, ABOVE The re-created late Renaissance garden at Moseley Old Hall, Wolverhampton, Staffordshire, was laid out in 1963. In the background is a tunnel arbour inspired by one depicted in Thomas Hill's *The Gardener's Labyrinth* (1577), with a vine, *Clematis viticella* and *C. flammula* growing over it. In the foreground is a re-creation of a garden of 1640, with box-edged beds and gravel paths. The beds have been filled with coloured gravels for low maintenance but in the original design they would have contained flowers.

OPPOSITE, BELOW The Jardin de la Saude, at Aix-en-Provence in France, is a re-creation laid out in about 1955, of a compartment from a late sixteenth-century château garden, a labyrinth of box with gravel walks. Patterns designed to be viewed from both house and terrace were a feature that remained central to garden design throughout the sixteenth and seventeenth centuries.

LEFT A recent re-creation of a late sixteenth-century knot at Barnsley House, Gloucestershire, has two identical knots, each 12 ft (3.66 m) square, made up of green and golden box intertwined with a lozenge of germander, with a dome of *Phillyrea angustifolia* at the centre. The pattern is taken from the 1583 edition of *L'Agriculture et Maison Rustique*. Knots can be scaled up or down and may be filled with either coloured gravels or flowers. Rosemary, thyme, santolina or marjoram would be more correct – if more labour-intensive – alternatives to box, which came into use only after about 1620.

and squares reflected the true reality of God, while the wild wood or parkland beyond, by contrast, was evidence of the results of man's estrangement from his creator at the Fall. In response to this principle, gardens began to be reordered into geometric spaces, to be experienced by the visitor as a sequence of different compartments. These were arranged along one or more axes, and unity was lent to the whole by the use of vistas and sophisticated directional impulses, such as a fountain or a mount. Another fundamental change was in the

approach to the relationship of house and garden, which were now viewed as a series of interconnecting spaces radiating from the house. Gardens had to be ordered, and at some point that order had to be visible at a glance either from the upper windows of the house or from a terrace beneath them. It was the architect Bramante (*c.* 1444-1514) who in 1503, inspired by classical precedent, linked the Villa Belvedere to the Vatican by means of a series of terraces and flights of steps down a hillside, and who in so doing invented garden architecture.

When the Elizabethan traveller Fynes Moryson visited the Villa Medici in Rome in 1594, he recorded the three main elements of a Renaissance garden: 'And the first garden had onely flowers; the second in the upper part, had a sweet Grove, and the lower part was full of fruit trees.' As in the Middle Ages,

gardens were enclosed by a wall or hedge, which would usually be about 5 to 7 feet (1.7 to 2.3 metres) high and composed either of a mixture of shrubs and trees or of one plant only, such as juniper. Walls would be clothed with vines and other climbing plants and espaliered fruit trees. Hedged geometric enclosures or *compartimenti* would meanwhile be filled with fruit trees, and often bounded by low hedges of sage, rosemary or lavender. Gravel walks between them might be accentuated by pergolas or tunnel arbours (a surviving medieval feature) of pleached willow or mulberry. Finally, near the house, was the *orto*, consisting of beds in various geometric patterns containing flowers and herbs, planted at random and with no concern either for repeat patterns or for the varying heights of the plants. Throughout these gardens were containers in abundance: large terracotta pots, filled notably with shrubs such as orange and lemon trees and dotted along parapets and around fountains. To these basic elements the more elaborate gardens added further ones which were in the main the result of the renewed study and emulation of classical antiquity: symbolic statuary, grottoes, mounts, tree houses, topiary and, above all, water. More than ever this was to become the uniting factor in garden-making, as it was persuaded by ever more elaborate contrivances to shoot upwards, cascade downwards, spurt sideways and drip and trickle in all directions.

All of these developments were to cross the Alps after 1500, gradually re-shaping the gardens of northern Europe, first in France and then steadily across the continent. In France château gardens began to be laid out in geometric compartments, but generally away from the dwelling. Not until the middle of the century did the two begin to become united into a single symmetrical whole. Grand waterworks, statuary and grottoes were slow to percolate northwards.

What is more significant for our small garden quest is the emergence of an illustrated literature of garden design aimed at those who lived in the small manors and farmhouses of France and England. *L'Agriculture et Maison Rustique* (1564) by Charles Estienne and Jean Liébault, for example, which ran through four editions, described a modest country estate with an axial broadwalk dividing the potager from the parterre or flower garden, which in turn led on to the orchard. Each section was surrounded by a hedge and within that was sub-divided, if possible, by *berceaux* or tunnel arbours of trellis covered with climbers such as musk roses and jasmine. The parterre itself was then divided into two equal parts, one

planted with flowers for cutting and the other mainly with fragrant species for scent. The flower garden was further sub-divided into square compartments, each of which was to contain a knot laid out in pennyroyal, wild thyme, sage, rosemary, hyssop, camomile, violets, daisies or basil, within containing borders of lavender, rosemary or box.

The designs suggested for knots were copied all over Europe, and were pirated by Thomas Hill for his *Gardener's Labyrinth* (1577), one of a number of books which gives us an insight into the design of late Tudor and Jacobean gardens. From these and surviving documentation it is clear that on the whole northern Europe did not respond to the full implications of the Italian garden revolution until well into the middle of the seventeenth century.

ABOVE The re-created French Renaissance *jardin-potager* at Villandry, Indre-sur-Loire, France, was a pioneer attempt, laid out between 1906 and 1924. This view looks down over one of the nine geometrically patterned squares based on engravings of ground-plans of late sixteenth-century château gardens. The symmetrically arranged beds, filled with produce and flowers and enclosed within a lattice-work fence, are authentically of the period; the central urn and the use of box to edge the beds are not.

OPPOSITE The botanic garden at the University of Leiden, the Netherlands, re-created in 1990, is laid out to two-thirds of the scale of the original, which was started in 1594 under the supervision of the celebrated botanist Charles de l'Ecluse, or Clusius. The plants are displayed for teaching purposes in long rectangular beds laid out in a grid system, with a decorative arch at the garden's central crossing point.

A LATE MEDIEVAL GARDEN

All the exquisite quality of a manuscript illumination is evoked in this garden, over which the eye is asked to wander and drink in every detail. The medieval gardens that we know about were simple yet highly sophisticated; recorded with meticulous accuracy in contemporary illustrations, the Flemish gardens of the fifteenth century encompass the essential common factors which add up to make a style. They were small and inward-looking, and so would suit both country and urban sites. In layout they were formal, and their design was about enclosure: outer walls or wattle fences, and inner lattice-work low fences allowing access to rectangular raised beds held in by wood or brick. The plant range was extremely limited; each flower was to be viewed in isolation and with wonder; and there was no sculpture apart from simple fountains into which water reluctantly spouted.

In this plan I have deliberately divided the space into two in order to give expression to the main types of garden – or 'herber' as they were known – typical of the close of the Middle Ages. One contains raised beds arranged with quite a high degree of formality, while the other is a flowery mead whose essence is a sophisticated and studied naturalism, achieved

A simple turf seat with a wooden arbour supporting the ancient crimson apothecary's rose, *Rosa gallica officinalis*, enlivens a corner of the garden. The container of trained rosemary would be moved around the garden, but the seat itself could be planted, for instance with *Lilium candidum*.

through seemingly artless informality. Together they provide a delightful contrast, with the symmetry and geometry of the raised beds making a graceful transition between the house and the apparently wild garden beyond. Although medieval gardens were generally flat enclosures without changes of level, they were often reached down a flight of steps from the bedroom of the lady of the house. This reflected both a keen appreciation of horizontal pattern in the garden, best viewed from above (knots had become fashionable by the close of the fifteenth century), and a desire for ready access.

The raised bed herber is based on similar ones depicted in many paintings of the period, including those illustrated overleaf, and depends heavily on structure. For modern gardeners perhaps the most unaccustomed element in the garden, both visually and horticulturally, is the turf that fills virtually all the beds, which should be studded with topiary (which was often curiously supported and tied into place), shrubs and flowers. Exceptionally, a bed may be filled with flowers of a single species supported by a lattice-work frame.

The design for the flowery mead herber is inspired by the many late medieval paintings depicting the Virgin and Child seated among the lush, flower-studded grass (see page 20). It might be tempting to imagine that this is the easier of the two gardens both to make and to maintain. In fact the reverse is true. Great care would need to be exercised in cutting the grass in order to keep it at just the right length, let alone ensuring that the flowers strewn among it multiply. This is a more delicate matter than it sounds, as wild flowers will not thrive in competition with grass which will soon take over on ordinary garden soil. The answer is to impoverish the ground by stripping off the topsoil and planting directly into the subsoil. In the Middle Ages the maintenance of a flowery mead would have been a highly labour-intensive process, involving flowers being planted into the grass season by season. My own approach would be to make this into a largely springtime garden and cheat by using bulbs such as narcissi, crocus, Lent lilies and fritillaries (but not tulips); you could also plant colchicums and *Crocus sativus* for interest later in the year. I would then leave the grass, cutting it just before the roses tumble over the lattice-work fence. Asymmetry is crucial to the success of this herber: plants and artefacts – a large turf bench, a fountain, fruit trees, roses and an estrade tree (an elaborately trained tree pruned into tiers) – are dotted about at will, bearing in mind the needs of the plants.

The garden is about 70 x 40 ft (21.3 x 12.2 m), and divided into two areas: the raised bed herber, enclosed by lattice-work fencing, measures about 40 ft (12.2 m) square; and the flowery mead herber through the doorway measures about 30 x 40 ft (9.1 x 12.2 m). The wall on the left faces south-east, and the design assumes a little more land beyond the far fence to accommodate toolshed, compost heap and bonfire patch.

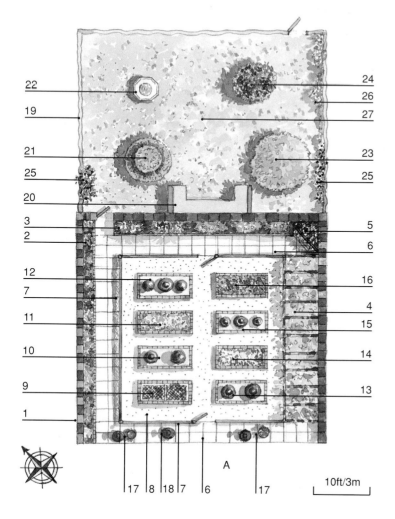

THE RAISED BED HERBER

The herber is enclosed by a handsome crenellated brick wall (**1**) about 6 ft (1.8 m) high, with indentations low enough to be looked over. A quickthorn hedge would be as correct for this period, though somewhat prone to disease. Against the south-east-(**2**) and south-west- (**3**) facing walls are narrow raised beds of brick, planted with flowers of the period spaced about 3 ft (90 cm) apart. It is important to choose flowers which will give a bold silhouette against the brick wall, such as foxgloves, irises, Canterbury bells and Madonna lilies. The north-west facing tunnel arbour (**4**) is of carpenter's work, stained with preservative and covered with vines *(Vitis vinifera)* to give summer shade and autumn fruits. In the west-facing corner is a raised turf seat (**5**) under a simple rustic pergola (see previous page). The central garden is surrounded by a stone or slab path (**6**) and enclosed by a low lattice-work fence (**7**). Here the fence is stained with a preservative, but in the period it was popular to paint them white. Within the enclosure of gravel or sand (**8**) are eight raised brick beds, (**9-16**) one or

two courses high and measuring 6 x 4 ft (1.8 x 1.2 m). Wooden planks would be an appropriate alternative to the brick. The beds can be treated in a variety of ways, but it is important to include topiary in bay, holly, rosemary or any other evergreen plant known in the period, to give the composition vital and constant vertical accents. In this scheme (**9**) is planted with dianthus supported by a trellis-work frame; (**10**) has topiary bay and box in turf; (**11**) is covered in thyme; (**12**) has two topiary hollies flanking a box; (**13**) has bay and box clipped as cake-stands, which could be underplanted with pot marigolds; (**14**) contains turf dappled with ox-eye daisies; (**15**) has topiary crataegus and holly; and (**16**) has violets growing through the turf. Containers, often filled with tender plants, were also very popular, and in summer would be dotted around on both the beds and the turf seats. Here they are placed on the terrace which runs in front of the house (**A**), and contain dianthus (**17**) supported in the period manner – probably with pliable willow lashed together – and more topiary (**18**).

THE FLOWERY MEAD HERBER

This is enclosed by a wattle fence 3 or 4 ft (90 or 120 cm) high (**19**), of a type available today, and treated with a preservative. The turf seat (**20**) is supported by the wall; the estrade tree (**21**), perhaps a holly or a small deciduous tree such as a pear, is the result of a curious piece of training, involving pruning and tying the branches to wooden hoops in order to make something akin

to a leafy umbrella. The contemporary illuminations that depict this practice are so precise that, with secateurs to hand and a certain amount of patience, a gardener could achieve this triumph of the medieval topiarist's art without too much difficulty. Typically it would be growing out of a double bank held in by wattle, as seen in the period illustration opposite; the fountain (**22**) is optional, although the sound of moving water always brings pleasure, and reconstituted stone ones in the Gothic style are available today; for such a small area the fruit tree (**23**) needs to be of dwarf rootstock, giving a mature tree of some 12 ft (3.6 m) in diameter at the crown. I would suggest a medlar *(Mespilus germanica)*, for the beauty of its lustrous ochre and auburn autumn foliage; or a quince *(Cydonia oblonga)*, which bears fragrant golden autumn fruits. The single rose (**24**) that emerges from a wattle-enclosed raised bed is the ancient *Rosa* 'Alba Semiplena', the white rose of York, which can form a magnificent arching bush 8ft (2.4 m) high, with the bonus of bright red hips in autumn. The parti-coloured Rosa Mundi or *Rosa gallica* 'Versicolor'(**25**), and honeysuckle *(Lonicera periclymenum)* (**26**) are trained over the fence, bringing added interest and scent to the herber in the summer. The turf (**27**) should be planted with primroses, daisies, forget-me-nots, violets, daffodils, cowslips, snowdrops, speedwell, buttercups, wild strawberries and cornflowers, although my suggestions for bulbs, while not strictly authentic, would be easier to maintain.

LEFT A French illumination of a walled town herb garden, *c.*1485, divided into square beds, each one filled with a particular herb. The low beds must have been boarded in and the paths between sanded. Near the house is a circular well for watering. The plan is a very typical one.

RIGHT A view of a Netherlandish garden *c.*1490 from a summerhouse back towards the main house. The raised rectangular beds are of brick with sanded paths in between. The bed in the left foreground has carnations supported by trellis while to the right a bed of lavender is held in by rails. Others are filled with trimmed estrade trees and shrubs arising from turf. Notice the flowers in containers on the bed to the right and the typical support for a plant, left.

ABOVE A tall trained estrade tree from a French manuscript, 1501–07, with tiered turf seats at its base held in by wattle fencing . The branches are clipped and entwined onto a series of fanciful circular frames.

AN ITALIAN RENAISSANCE GARDEN

The Italian Renaissance garden is one of the great and, at the same time, most acceptable of all classic garden styles. Its basis is simply the ordered, geometric division of space – however large or small. Our knowledge of the style is based chiefly on the great villa gardens, but because they were divided into several enclosed rectangular spaces – known as *compartimenti* – it is possible, by selecting and reducing the number of *compartimenti*, to evoke an Italian Renaissance garden on a far smaller scale. I have included here three of the essential components of any such garden: an enclosure with fruit trees – with the added period interest of a tunnel arbour; a *bosco* or wood; and an *orto* or decorative pattern of beds filled with herbs and flowers placed close to the house. Each one in itself would make a complete and delightfully unusual garden.

The design is derived from elements to be found in a series of fourteen paintings of the Medici villas in 1599 by the Flemish artist Giusto Utens. It draws in particular on the villas Poggio, La Ambrogiana and La Petraia, all of which are laid out in a geometric grid of squares and rectangles with enclosing walls or hedges, within which are tunnel arbours, trees planted in patterns, geometric beds, and shrubs in terracotta tubs. Following the Renaissance emphasis on the importance of changes of level – in order to provide sweeping views and pleasant prospects – it is ideally a garden for a south-facing slope, but it could, of course, be laid out on the flat. Here the *orto*, the geometric beds containing herbs and flowers, is given its traditional position as the garden nearest the house, its strong pattern observable from the windows of the *piano nobile*. It lies on a terrace behind the house so that herbs and flowers are close at hand for both culinary purposes and

general delight. Below this there stretches the main orchard garden, with its vine-covered tunnel arbours to provide the shade that is essential in a south-facing garden and a central pavilion of greenery in which to sit on hot days. Each fruit tree stands in the middle of a square of grass enclosed by a fragrant rosemary hedge. The south-facing wall gives an opportunity to make a major architectural statement, while the east and west walls support espaliered fruit trees planted in beds wide enough to contain roses and other flowers.

On the western terrace is a dramatic and densely planted miniature *boschetto*, or small wood, mostly of evergreens. If you have the space to make a larger *bosco*, simply multiply the enclosures, repeating both the size and the formula. And why not add a bed with your initials in topiary as the grand dukes of Tuscany did, in imitation of the ancient custom mentioned by Pliny the Younger in his letters describing his own villa garden in the first century AD? Although box did not come into extensive use until the next century it was already utilized for topiary, as Pliny confirms, and I suggest it here for its permanence.

This is not an excessively labour-intensive or expensive garden. The fruit trees will require training and pruning, as will the vines over the arbours; and the amount of attention required by your *orto* lies entirely in your hands: a planting of long-lived herbs would reduce it to a minimum. The greatest expense would obviously be the landscaping and building work, but costly balustrading can be replaced with an equally authentic lattice-work fence clothed with climbing plants; and while the containers dotted along the walls are an enhancement, they are not essential.

Between the flights of steps that lead down from a terrace is an arched recess housing a simple mask and basin wall fountain. Rendered walls with courses of tiles are a more attractive alternative for the steps and parapet than balustrading, which tends to to look eighteenth rather than sixteenth century; simple iron railings or painted wooden lattice-work would be as suitable.

The orchard garden with its shade-giving tunnel arbour measures about 80 ft
(24.4 m) square, and looks out towards the south. It is one part of a roughly
L-shaped garden; on the two terraces above and out of view are a *bosco*
(or wood) and the *orto* (or geometric flower garden).

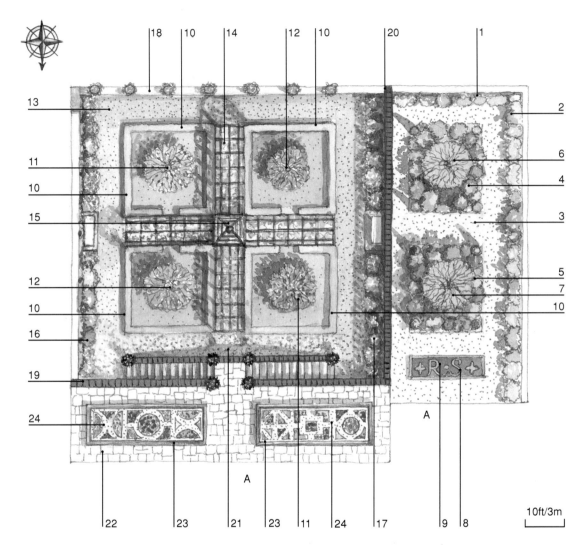

fruit tree. Here there are two peaches (**11**) and two almonds: (**12**); if you want to use apples or pears I would suggest using modern dwarf rootstock, which produces trees about 12 ft (3.6 m) in diameter at the crown. You could, if climate allows, choose something more exotic, perhaps a pomegranate *(Punica granatum)* or a medlar *(Mespilus germanica)*. The enclosures are surrounded and separated by gravel walks (**13**). The garden in dominated by vine-covered tunnel arbours 8 ft (2.4 m) high (**14**), with a central pavilion rising to about 12 ft (3.6 m) high (**15**). Ideally the construction should be of carpenter's work, however rough, and the wood stained dark with preservative. Ready-made steel arcading is available and would do, but avoid a black plastic finish at all costs. To the vines, which provide summer shade and autumn colour, you might like to add honeysuckle *(Lonicera caprifolium)* and clematis *(Clematis flammula)* for their scent and flowers. In the west-facing (**16**) and east-facing (**17**) narrow beds are espaliered or fan-trained cherry, peach, apricot and fig trees growing against the walls, which are washed creamy white. In the spaces between I would suggest a planting to include Madonna lilies, hollyhocks and roses: *RR.× damascena, × centifolia* and *gallica*. The southern wall (**18**) is low, with a view over the landscape, and is wide enough to bear terracotta pots, ideally holding orange and lemon trees. The retaining walls to the north (**19**) and the west (**20**) are 8 ft (2.4 m) high and rendered. They could be topped by classical balustrading, which is readily available in a reconstituted stone. Flights of steps lead up to the *orto*

10ft/3m

THE *BOSCO* OR WOOD

This is walled or hedged in with narrow borders to the south (**1**) and west (**2**) containing mostly evergreen shrubs: laurel, crataegus and *Viburnum tinus,* with ivy on the walls. Gravel walks (**3**) surround two large enclosures, 20 x 24 ft (6 x 7.3 m), densely planted with trees and shrubs (**4** and **5**). At the centre of each is a large specimen tree (**6** and **7**) such as a plane

(Platanus orientalis), or holm oak *(Quercus ilex).* The corners are emphasized by Italian cypresses and the space between is filled with shrubs including laurel, broom *(Cytisus scoparius),* lilac *(Syringa vulgaris), Daphne mezereum,* dogwood *(Cornus sanguinea)* and myrtle *(Myrtus communis).* Close to the house (**A**) I have suggested a topiary bed with the owner's initials in clipped box (**8**) or rosemary, against a

ground of stone chippings or coloured gravels (**9**).

THE ORCHARD GARDEN

This area contains four plots 24 ft (7.3 m) square, and enclosed within a hedge (**10**) of rosemary, sage or lavender, kept clipped to about 1 ft 6 ins (45 cm) high. The enclosures are planted with grass, which you could treat as a flowery mead and plant with spring flowers (see pages 30-33). At the centre of each square is a

or flower garden, on the terrace above; they flank a central wall fountain (**21**) (see previous page).

THE *ORTO*, OR GARDEN OF HERBS AND FLOWERS

This garden can be elaborated or simplified according to taste. A stone-flagged or slabbed terrace (**22**) in front of the house (**A**) holds two rectangular areas, 32 x 12 ft (9.7 x 3.6 m), enclosed by clipped lavender hedges (**23**). Within these enclosures are beds – each of a different geometric pattern – set in gravel (**24**), their edges defined by planks (better still would be a course of bricks, but ribbons of low-growing herbs such as santolina could also be used). Generally each bed would contain a single type of plant, with no regard for relative heights, nor planted to make repeat patterns. In summer containers, ideally with orange or lemon trees, can be added in order to accentuate the geometry.

LEFT Two of the four main *compartimenti* at the Medici Villa Ambrogiana in 1599. Each is contained by clipped hedges. Within the hedges each area is divided into geometric boarded-in beds. Notice the arbitrary incorporation of trees and that each bed is filled with a single plant with no attention paid to the variations in height. To the right, oblong beds contain the owner's name in topiary.

BELOW Part of the garden of the Medici Villa Petraia as planted in 1591-7. The Renaissance system of geometric *compartimenti* here takes the form of a square quartered by paths and transversed by two circular wooden tunnel arbours or pergolas. Clipped hedges define the quarters; two of the spandrels are densely planted with trees as *boschetti*; the other trees are evenly spaced and planted in circles, to echo the lines of the tunnel arbours. Trees are trained up against the retaining wall at the back, which has a simple wall fountain and bowl in the centre.

ABOVE The alternative design for a circular tunnel arbour is inspired by the famous pair at the Medici Villa Petraia, constructed in the last quarter of the sixteenth century. In the middle is a pond with a single water jet, surrounded by a parapet wide enough to take plants in terracotta pots.

A NORTHERN RENAISSANCE GARDEN

This is a garden of a kind that Shakespeare would have known. It retains the medieval love of detail and enclosure but adds to it a Renaissance sense of order. The repetition of a series of identical enclosed geometric spaces is critical to evoking a type of layout which spread through France, Germany, the Low Countries and England from the 1580s onwards in response to the new ideas of the Italian Renaissance. Encompassed by a hedge of quickthorn, the standard hedging plant of the age, it includes a hornbeam tunnel arbour (a medieval feature which lived on); a flower garden planted with flowers for seasonal colour and evergreen topiary and hedging for year-round interest; and a potager divided into compartments containing vegetable beds, a small orchard and a herb garden.

The potager is a simplified version of the many garden patterns in the Dutch artist Vredemann de Vries's *Hortorum Viridariorumque elegantes et multiplices formae...* (Antwerp, 1583), which was influential throughout northern Europe. Its most distinctive feature is the woodwork which would give instant, unmistakeable period effect even though the capital outlay would be high. The Renaissance emphasis on symmetry and formality rules out any softening of hard contours by allowing plants to tumble over them, but there is ample room here for fruit trees, soft fruit, vegetables and herbs.

The flower garden is based on one of several designs in Salomon de Caus's *Les Raisons des Forces Mouvantes* (1615), combined with elements from one of Crispin de Passe's most famous engravings illustrated overleaf. While not complicated to maintain, this garden calls for patience, as the hedges and topiary require between five and eight years to mature – unless you use fully grown specimens.

The atmosphere of introspection is emphasized by the tunnel arbour – a medieval feature which retained its vitality into the 1680s – and another, inner wall or hedge, here of beech. Standard hollies stand at the corners and entrances, presenting a striking contrast in winter to the russet leaves of the beech. Squares and rectangles of smooth turf continue the medieval tradition of appreciating grass for its own special beauties, and form a containing band of restful areas of green, with cypresses acting as stately sentinels in the corners. The flowerbeds in the centre are edged with clipped box, and are filled with topiary and flowers which, to be correct, would be sparsely planted. I would cheat and make it denser, but avoid any suggestion of anachronistic bedding out.

The garden on the south-facing side of the house consists of two identical
compartments, a flower garden and a potager, each 60 ft (18.3 m) square. The
containing hedge should be high enough to protect the garden from wind and
cold, but low enough to allow the sun to cross it, and could be trimmed into
simple geometric shapes – such as crenellations if desired. The design assumes
enough space to the north of the potager for an adjacent service area, where
practicalities such as a shed and compost heap can be housed.

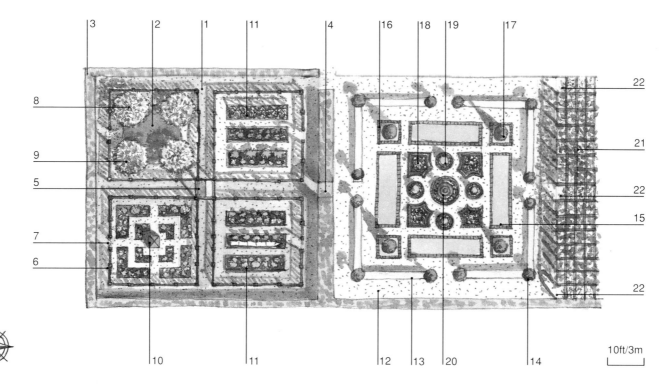

10ft/3m

THE POTAGER

The whole area would all have been gravelled (**1**), but to avoid monotony I would use grass under the fruit trees (**2**) and you could pave the herb garden with stones, brick or slabs. The quickthorn hedge (**3**) forms an arch (**4**) where it frames the entrance, and allows access to the rest of the garden. The central pavilion (**5**) and fencing can be as elaborate or as simple as you wish; these are based on the ones in the *Hortus Botanicus* of the great botanist Carolus Clusius (1526-1609) in Leiden. The central feature is an elegant mannerist confection painted a cream colour, but the columns could equally well be marbled and the finials gilded. Trellis-work could be used instead of the slatted fencing (**6**), which here is stained with a wood preservative but could as well be painted cream or green. Each of the four compartments

is 24 ft (7.3 m) square and approached through wooden arches (**7**), which again could be painted to match the central pavilion. The orchard (**2**) has a lawn and four dwarf rootstock fruit trees, here two pears (**8**) and two apples (**9**). The herb garden has a topiary bay pyramid (**10**) at its centre. To be authentic, it should be planted with space between each herb; but as it would be impossibly constraining to plant the vegetable and the soft fruit areas (**11**) in the correct period manner, I have left them to be filled strictly according to the requirements of today's cook in beds that are raised and retained by either planks or bricks, as in the Middle Ages.

THE FLOWER GARDEN

A broad gravelled walk some 6 ft (1.8 m) wide (**12**) surrounds an enclosing hedge of beech (**13**). Standard hollies (**14**) mark the corners and entrances.

Training these takes a long time: even yew would be quicker, and if you are really impatient you could train leaders up from the beech and cut them into finials. Inside the hedge are four rectangular (**15**) and four square (**16**) areas of turf, slightly raised and edged with brick, and with Italian cypresses (**17**) at the corners (for colder climates the only acceptable alternative is the modern columnar juniper 'Skyrocket'). The flowerbeds, which are also raised with brick, are edged with box (**18**), though thyme, germander or santolina would be suitable alternatives. Variegated box (**19**) and yew (**20**) topiary give vertical accents. The spring planting within the beds is of crown imperials, Roman hyacinths and 'Rembrandt' tulips (bulbs have changed so much over the centuries that the best anyone can do is plant what looks as

right as possible); it could be followed by pansies, pot marigolds, *Dianthus caryophyllus*, Canterbury bells and *Crocus sativus*.

THE TUNNEL ARBOUR

Made of stained wood, the construction of the arbour (**21**) is open to elaboration or simplification according to preference and resources. It would take about eight years to prune and train the hornbeam right over it, but the results would be unforgettable, a showpiece in which to sit, eat, walk or work. The three entrances (**22**) should be entwined with sweet-smelling climbing roses and honeysuckle, as in the de Passe engraving (see opposite). A seat placed in the centre would enable you to enjoy the view through to the potager. If you have views to look out towards on the other side, make 'windows' in the tunnel.

BELOW A garden of 1606 shows the division of space into squares: in front are two knots enclosed with hedges and planted with flowers, and beyond is a fountain with edged beds around it. Behind is an igloo-like arbour, probably of pleached trees over a wooden frame

ABOVE An alternative, far more ambitious, way of treating the central area of flowerbeds would be to make a knot. These had reached their heyday in the sixteenth century, and by 1620 were already going out of fashion in the great gardens. The two designs above are taken from Thomas Hill's *The Gardener's Labyrinth* (1577), and could be laid out in dwarf box, santolina and germander, or in three varieties of box (green, golden and variegated) which would at least be permanent rather than needing to be renewed periodically, as the santolina and germander. Knots were treated in one of two ways: one way was to plant the earth between with a sprinkling of flowers through the seasons; the other was to infill the spaces with coloured gravels or chippings, sand or brick dust arranged in a pattern. Ground bones and coal dust would be as authentic but perhaps less acceptable today.

ABOVE In a Netherlandish spring flower garden engraved by Crispin de Passe in *Hortus Floridus* (1616), the geometric patterned beds are enclosed by a low edging plant, perhaps clipped thyme, and have small topiary shrubs as focal points and vertical accents. The widely-spaced plants include tulips, hyacinths and crown imperials. A wooden tunnel arbour planted with rose and honeysuckle contains the composition.

LEFT A small garden at Trinity College, Cambridge, 1688. By then very old-fashioned, it consists of raised turf beds arranged in a symmetrical pattern and planted with junipers and flowering shrubs, contained by a shrubby hedge. There is what seems to be a fruit tree trained against the house.

Age of Display

1620~1720

Dominance in garden design passed from Italy to France in the seventeenth century, and was epitomized in the work of one great creative genius, André Le Nôtre (1613-1700). This was the golden age of absolutism in Europe, when gardens came to express the submission of the world of nature to man, and especially to monarchs. Whereas the vistas and perspectives of the Renaissance garden met in the eyes of man, in the baroque age which followed those eyes were to become royal ones. Only in the king's gaze could the design of such gardens find their true fulfilment and meaning.

A painting by an unknown artist, showing the garden of Pierrepont House, Nottingham, as it was some thirty years after it was laid out in 1677, provides us with a rare record of the delights of a late seventeenth-century town garden. The ground-plan is quartered and each quarter is laid out in identical patterns. Set into grass, which was enormously labour-intensive to maintain, all the beds are edged with stone and filled with flowers. All the available wall space is given over to espaliered fruit trees, while the plethora of plant containers would have been brought out for the summer months only.

The Wilderness at Ham House, Richmond, Surrey, re-created in 1976-7, was originally laid out in the 1670s. Wildernesses, part of the repertory of the formal style that has now been lost, were geometric plantings of hedges and small trees, forming avenues, vistas and 'rooms' in which to stroll and sit. The hedge here is of hornbeam (*Carpinus betulus*). During the summer handsome wooden seats painted white would be placed in the alcoves and arbours, and plants in Versailles tubs would be added to the composition.

This represented a gigantic revolution in ways of looking and in the manipulation of space, which was accompanied by parallel developments in the individual elements of garden composition. These changes began in France with the work of the Mollet family: Claude (*fl.*1595-1610) laid out the gardens of Henri IV and was responsible for a crucial step in the evolution of that quintessential element of the seventeenth-century garden, the parterre. Evergreen clipped box now reigned supreme and at the same time garden compartments, formerly a series of separate and different knots, were united by means of repeating and reversing a single pattern. The next step was probably taken by Jacques Boyceau (*d. c.* 1633), who planned the vast parterre for the French queen Marie de Medici's new palace of the Luxembourg (1615). Planted to be viewed from the state apartments on the *piano nobile*, this was a vast evergreen swirling carpet of pattern, anticipating the baroque style in its rhythms. The box was set against coloured grounds, and the whole was surrounded by an artificial terrace around which to stroll and from which to contemplate its magnificence.

This was the milestone which signalled the triumph of French garden style under Louis XIV and which was ensured by the two great gardening dynasties, the Mollets and the Le Nôtres. André Mollet (*d.c.* 1665) took the style to England, the Netherlands and Sweden. André Le Nôtre provided the world with its greatest exemplar, Versailles (begun 1661), destined to be copied with variations in countries as far apart as Russia and Spain. Although starting to fall out of fashion by 1750, it needed the French Revolution to render both the style and the political system it epitomized obsolete.

What is astonishing is how many of these grand palace gardens in the French style have survived, albeit changed. Apart from Versailles itself there is Le Nôtre's perhaps greater masterpiece, Vaux-le-Vicomte, Seine-et-Marne (completed 1661). In the Netherlands the French designer, Daniel Marot (1661-1752) laid out the garden of Het Loo, Apeldoorn, Guelderland (begun 1685), which has recently been restored to its former splendour. The rulers of the small German states created a succession of minature Versailles; and the first Bourbon kings took the style to Spain. Le Nôtre himself provided designs in England for both Greenwich (*c.* 1663) and Windsor (1698). George London (*d.*1714) and Henry Wise (1653-1738) spread the manner in England albeit with a Netherlandish accent, laying out the gardens of Hampton Court (begun 1689) and Kensington Palace (begun 1691).

More surprising was its export to the New World, not only

The canal and elegant summerhouse in the garden at Westbury Court, Westbury-upon-Severn, Gloucestershire, laid out between 1696 and 1705, bear witness to the importation of the narrow Dutch canal as a garden feature, prized for its ability to emphasize perspective, catch the light and reflect garden buildings in its calm waters. The restoration of this garden (begun in 1971), was one of the earliest attempts at accurate re-creation, based on extensive archival documentation. The yew hedges have cones and balls of holly rising from them, and espaliered fruit trees are planted against the long brick wall.It is quite possible to achieve a similar effect on a smaller scale and with a much more modest garden building, but using the basic elements of the building, the long, narrow reflective ribbon of water and the clipped evergreens (see page 56).

ABOVE A re-creation from the 1980s of a small manor house garden in Gwent, Wales, of the late seventeenth century shows extensive use of carpenter's work for vertical accents. The woodwork is of a kind which no longer survives but for which the designs are to be found in Jan van der Groen's *Den Nederlandtsen Hovenier* (1659) (see page 57).

OPPOSITE A detail of the *plate-bande* in the re-created King's Garden of the palace of Het Loo, Apeldoorn, the Netherlands, begun in 1685 and re-created in 1984. The box-edged border encircles the parterre, and clipped yew cones provide vertical accents. The white sand outside the border is designed to catch the box clippings. Within it is a spring planting of tulips, crown imperials and hyacinths in orange and blue, the colours of William III.

to French colonies such as Louisiana, but also, modulated by Dutch and English influences, to New England. London and Wise sent the designs and a gardener to supervise the gardens of William and Mary College (begun 1694) in Williamsburg, the new capital of Virginia. Since 1926 the gardens of this historic town have been restored, giving today's gardeners a more accessible and domestic version of a style which now survives only at grand palaces in Europe.

These are a salutary reminder that the style affected thousands of quite modest gardens round the smaller houses of the period, laid out in a much simplified and reduced version of what started as palatial grandeur. The design elements and the approach, however, were always the same, and began with a great change in ideas about the siting of houses. While the

Renaissance villa had stood on a south-facing terraced hillside, the seventeenth-century house was set in a valley on as flat a site as could be found.

Around the house the garden was laid out on a grid system, always respecting a grand central axis, and generally with the sections on one side of the axis mirroring those on the other exactly. Changes of level were generally subtle rather than dramatic, being confined to terraces and connecting flights of steps. Bird's-eye views of these gardens show them as a series of squares and rectangles imposed on the landscape. The result was assertive and through the device of using avenues of trees to continue the garden's vistas this assertiveness was extended across the surrounding countryside.

The garden moved through a progression from the back or sides of the house: immediately beneath the first-floor windows was laid out its *chef d'oeuvre*, the parterre. By the close of the century the parterre had become so complex that a whole repertory of names had been devised to denote the various types, ranging from the *parterre de broderie*, that is box scrollwork in elaborate repeat patterns against coloured grounds, to the simpler *parterre à l'angloise*, green turf cut into patterns and perhaps set against sand with a statue or urn as a focal point. The parterre was the great showpiece, often surrounded by raised terraces or enclosed by a *plate-bande* of flowers, and animated by fountains and statuary. Like so many other elements of baroque design, however, it can be scaled down to the smallest space.

Beyond it lay the *bosquet* or wilderness. This again was a series of compartments planted in geometric shapes and patterns which, like the parterre, developed to embrace a highly sophisticated repertory, ranging from groves to mazes. Basically its effects were achieved by using hedges to form walks and enclosures, which could then be enlivened with anything from a grand set-piece, such as an open-air theatre, to the simple delights of fruit trees planted in patterns among flowering and scented shrubs and climbers.

Besides this stress on enclosure and suprise, there was also a preocupation with vistas. Every avenue led to something: a statue, a column, an arch or the house itself. Most intersections were similarly marked. Water became another essential element, with fountains as focal points and still sheets of water, known as *miroirs d'eau*, reflecting the sky, the house or a garden building in a manner which has never been surpassed.

But what of the planting? The overall effect would have

been of countless restless greens, both clipped and unclipped, forming a wonderful foil to the built elements, statues, steps, terraces, urns, vases, paths and other structures. Flowers were still precious and often extremely expensive. The New World was enriching the range, but in the seventeenth century a collection of plants was as prestigious and valuable as one of pictures. Each bloom was appreciated on a highly sophisticated level, and the *plate-bande* which encircled the parterre was viewed much as one would a gallery of Old Master paintings.

This was the age of tulipomania, when single bulbs changed hands at huge prices. The cultivation of exotic plants became a passion, expressed in the invention of greenhouses with stoves to heat them through the cold of winter. Flowers invaded the house as never before, not only in reality but also in the

lustrous flower pictures of the Dutch and Flemish Schools. Indeed house and garden became closely interlocked, and the patterns on the stucco, textiles and marquetry inside would have found their counterparts in the parterre designs outside, creating a unity which is impressive and still worth careful consideration today.

It was also the golden age of container gardening, though there was nothing haphazard about it, as in the Middle Ages and Renaissance. Terracotta, lead and ceramic containers full of carefully tended plants would be brought out for the summer months and placed with mathematical precision to add to the parterre's pattern; and orange and lemon trees in Versailles tubs were positioned to add rich and splendid vertical accents to the garden's composition.

The art of training reached its height during this century, never to be equalled afterwards. Topiary was carried out on a vast scale, and provided vital and constant vertical green structures. Hampton Court in its heyday (about 1700), for example, had over a thousand pieces to be clipped. At no other time were hedges used to such advantage in the control of space, providing walks and 'rooms', vistas and avenues. The kitchen garden likewise assumed the status of an art, under the influence of Jean-Baptiste de la Quintinie (1626-88), creator of the *potager du roi* at Versailles (1677-83). Fruit trees, for instance, were pruned into fans, palmettes, goblets, cordons or espaliers, giving aesthetic delight as well as better produce.

Trees were planted on a scale unknown since, with avenues of double, triple or even quadruple rows. Pattern-planting was

de rigeur, and the figure favoured above all others was the quincunx, with four trees making a square and a fifth at the centre. Simple effects, such as cutting a ride through a wood and lining it with a hornbeam hedge from which sprang standard trees, could add a note of magic. Or there was the cut, which gave the effect of opening up a vista by the strategy of trimming up old trees on either side to form an aerial hedge stretching into the distance. Training was incredibly inventive, making use of a tree trunk as a pillar, for example, and then tying and pruning the branches to form an arcade. These are effects which can be copied on quite a small scale.

Perhaps the most powerful of all lessons to be learned from these gardens is the importance of ground-level pattern and proportion. The latter was a Renaissance inheritance, based on the belief that harmony was achieved through mathematical ratios which automatically gave pleasure. By the close of the century this was even codified. If, for instance, the central path was 6 feet (1.8 metres) wide, the parterre quarter should be a ratio of that: twice at 12 feet (3.7 metres), three times at 18 feet (5.5 metres), or even four times at 24 feet (7.3 metres). But the multiple of four was never to be exceeded without a widening of the central path. This exactness accounts for the extraordinary satisfaction which we still derive from looking down on these gardens. It is also due to their subtle use of pattern and varieties of material, as the eye wanders over verdant turf, coloured gravels, green box, flowers, sand, brick, stone and water arranged in calming symmetry. Add to this changes of light and the seasons, and it is enough to remind us that before the plant boom of the last two hundred years people walked through and enjoyed gardens to the full for many reasons which render our own responses somewhat simplistic. As well as the beauties of the place, they could admire the art of the sculptor, of the topiarist, of the plant collector and of the hydraulic engineer.

Above all we should remember that to seventeenth-century eyes the garden was nature as it should be, tamed back to what it had been in the Garden of Eden before the Fall. The landscape beyond continued to be regarded as hazardous and hostile; only in the garden could a dialogue be held with the true world of nature, pruned and clipped into an order which reflected the reality of God's creation. In the period to come all of this was to be reversed, leading to the view still commonly held that formality and training are a distortion of nature. How surprised the creators of such gardens would have been.

ABOVE The gardening style that prevailed in seventeenth-century Europe continued in the United States throughout the following century. William Paca created his garden at Annapolis, Maryland, between 1765 and 1772. The garden here is a recreation from the late 1960s, though not based on archaeological evidence, of one of the elements that he might have used: a small boxwood parterre with 'plats' of grass lined with box, with brick edging and gravel walks. The standard roses are a doubtful addition.

LEFT and OPPOSITE Williamsburg, Virginia, was the state capital in the eighteenth century. Since 1926 its gardens have been re-created using mainly late seventeenth-century English garden manuals, and though the accuracy of these pioneer efforts might be questioned, there is no doubting their appeal. The garden on the left demonstrates the importance of produce in all early gardens: here espaliered apples are used to form railings round beds filled with vegetables and herbs. The picture opposite shows how carpentry, clipped evergreens and mature trees contributed to the overall effect.

A FRENCH CLASSICAL GARDEN

The most distinctive feature of the French classical garden style is the box parterre, planted in bold arabesques and designed to be looked down upon from the first-floor reception rooms, where its decorative pattern can be appreciated throughout the year. Even in the snowy depths of winter, the structure and sculptural qualities will give lasting pleasure. The style, with its *parterres de broderie* and clipped yew, fountains and allées, vistas and gravel walks, all laid out in the strictest symmetry, reached its apogee in the second half of the seventeenth century, and found its highest expression in the work of André Le Nôtre (1613-1700), whose masterpiece is the magnificent garden at Vaux-le-Vicomte. The design given here attempts to distil some of the elements of the Le Nôtre style into a very tiny area, in the full knowledge that this involves a contradiction in terms, as his genius lay in his orchestration of huge terrains. Happily one of those elements, the box parterre, can be utilized in the smallest of spaces with no loss of its supreme elegance, and in this design we see some of the principles of Le Nôtre's style applied to great effect in a small back garden: the central path laid out on axis with the house and running the entire length of the garden, the cross-axes, the use of water as a focal point, the importance of ground pattern to be viewed from above, and the considered use of statuary and sculpture.

Shown here is the classic formula of flowing scroll patterns in dwarf clipped box contained by low hedges, while finials on pedestals and clipped box cones provide vertical accents for the composition. The permanent fresh green of the box is emphasized by a ground of brick-coloured stones, gravel or dust, and the parterre as a whole is framed by paths of yellow gravel. The composition is further enlivened by a fountain which acts as a focal point. This can either be a single *jet d'eau* or a jet arising from a classically inspired figure. Changes of level between the different areas, however slight, immeasurably enhance the effect, and here shallow steps lead up to terraces at each end of the garden. The central vista is closed at the far end by a seat set within a simple arbour. This lies behind symmetrical 'wings' of hornbeam hedging which edge the terrace, and from which there grows a row of evenly spaced and clipped standard crataegus. Both of these provide a change in winter, as the crataegus is deciduous and the hornbeam turns to russet. Versailles tubs of clipped yew standards give added interest to the terrace. If the garden were wider, more tubs could be stationed at the extremities of the cross-axes of the walks, but always take care to respect the symmetry of the design. The

The classical Versailles tub, still available today. In its original form, the sides can be let down for root pruning and repotting and rings attached for supports to carry it out from the greenhouse to the garden. The late seventeenth century used these containers in a wholly original way: annually they invaded the garden bringing exotic vertical accents such as lemon and orange trees to enliven both terrace and parterre with further geometric pattern.

garden is contained within walls, washed creamy white in order to catch the light, which support espaliered fruit trees, and the bed that runs along the walls allows for a few period flowers.

The initial outlay for the construction work necessary for this type of scheme is fairly heavy, but thereafter both expense and upkeep are minimal. A less costly alternative would be to dispense with the water, but use a single large urn on a plinth as a focal point and replace the urns at the corners with Italian cypresses or box cones. Once the garden is established, the chief garden work will be an annual clipping and pruning, and, of course, the usual water garden requirements need to be met.

The box parterre was as fundamental a part of country garden design as it was of town gardens because it was almost always situated near the house, and this design can easily be adapted to form part of a larger scheme, as shown overleaf. At its simplest, the parterre could lead on to a low-maintenance orchard enclosed with a hedge and an avenue of clipped yews or small trees leading to the arbour. This type of layout can be seen today at the Château de Brécy in Calvados, France, a modest country house with a remarkable architectural garden, possibly laid out by François Mansart in the 1630s.

The ground-plans of a parterre can also be adapted to any rectangular or square shape and although usually divided into four equal parts they can also be designed as a simple double-image. To ensure good proportions, no quarter should exceed four times the width of the central path. Whatever changes you make, the central axis and the symmetry of the spaces and patterns are of crucial importance.

The garden is a rectangle 65 x 30 ft (19.8 x 9.1 m) stretching out from a north-facing wall. The box parterre, centred on the fountain, is at a slightly lower level than the terraces at either end, so that it can be looked down upon.

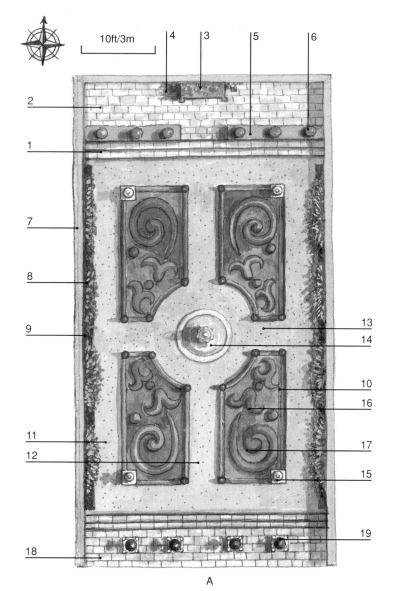

10ft/3m

A

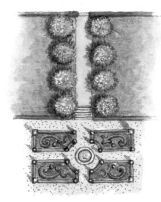

ABOVE An alternative way of using the parterre as part of a large garden would be to turn the design through 90° and use the cross axis as the main vista leading, perhaps, to an orchard or other space laid out on the same central axis to increase the sense of perspective.

ivy up it, but the result would be less correct. The walls are covered with espaliered or fan-trained fruit trees (**8**) which, depending on the aspect, could include pears, plums, peaches, apples, apricots or morello cherries, and beneath them are flowerbeds (**9**) which could hold a few period flowers. The parterre of clipped box (**10**) is surrounded by yellow gravel walks (**11**) about 4 ft (1.2 m) wide and quartered by a central (**12**) and a cross-axial (**13**) path. At the centre is a circular pond (**14**) with a retaining parapet and low sculptural fountain. Four finials (**15**), or urns on pedestals, hold the design at the four corners. These should be about 5 ft (1.5 m) high. The box scrolls (**16**) are clipped to give a gently rounded silhouette. If you are unsure about sculpting the curved and tapered shapes, grow all the box plants the same height, about 12 ins (30 cm), and clip the top flat and the sides straight, giving a more severe, but no less correct shape. The scrolls are set against a ground (**17**) of red brick dust, or coloured gravel or stone chippings. As a pretty, unusual, but far more labour-intensive, alternative you could create a flower garden by planting a

succession of seasonal flowers in the parterre in place of the coloured ground. To be in period, the flowers should be spot planted asymmetrically with no regard to varying heights or colours.

THE HOUSE TERRACE
The terrace (**18**) near the house (**A**) echoes the terrace at the other end of the garden, with steps leading down to the parterre. It is enlivened by four Versailles tubs containing topiary yew (**19**), which in warmer climates could be replaced with orange or lemon trees.

THE ARBOUR TERRACE
Shallow steps (**1**) lead up to a terrace (**2**) of stone or reconstituted Portland stone slabs. In the centre is a simple arbour (**3**) of carpenter's work painted blue-green. You may wish to soften its lines by growing a climber, such as a *Clematis cirrhosa* or honeysuckle (**4**) over it. Flanking hedges of hornbeam (**5**), 5 ft (1.5 m) high, have

standard crataegus (**6**) trained up through them. Yew is a possible alternative for the hedges, which also conceal a service area.

THE PARTERRE
The garden is enclosed by a wall 6 or 7 ft (about 2 m) high (**7**), which is rendered and painted a creamy white. If you have a fence you could cover it with trellis, painted the same blue-green as the arbour, and train

ABOVE An alternative pattern for one quarter of the parterre uses domes of box at the corners and contrasting coloured gravels or stone chippings to emphasize the bands of box, which are clipped with straight sides and flat top.

LEFT A turf *parterre à l'angloise* designed by André Le Nôtre at the Château de Conflans, *c.*1700. A simple form of garden-making in today's terms, the greensward was cut into a baroque pattern and set against gravel with topiary sentinels and a grand fountain at the end.

BELOW A diagram from Leonard Meager's *The English Gardener* (1670) shows four simple – for the period – alternative patterns for a box parterre. Each quarter would have been enclosed by a box hedge or a *plate-bande* (see page 55) with gravel as the ground for the central box patterns. The centre circle would have been either a fountain or grass with or without a statue.

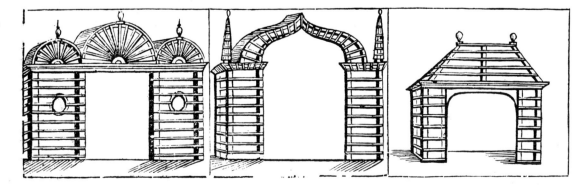

RIGHT Three designs for carpenter's work arches and arbours from Jan van der Groen's *Den Nederlandtsen Hovenier* (1669). These would have been painted and then had hornbeam or flowering climbers trained up and over them.

The garden is L-shaped and its overall extent of 90 x 130 ft (27.4 x 39.6 m) has made it possible to divide into three different areas: the canal garden is 80 x 50 ft (24.4 m x 39.6 m); the grove is 50 ft (15.2 m) square, and the turf parterre on the far side of the house 40 x 36 ft (12.2 x 11 m). The façade of the house overlooking the canal faces north, and the canal garden is raised about 3 ft (90 cm) above the parterre.

A 'WILLIAM AND MARY' GARDEN

This elegant garden makes use of the optical devices exported by the Dutch gardeners of the period to make it look far larger than it really is. It combines three of the main ingredients of the late seventeenth-century formal garden as it evolved in England and the Low Countries: a soft green turf parterre near the house; a canal, whose still waters reflect its surroundings and the changing skies above; and a grove, an inviting arrangement of trees, hedges and shrubs. The essence of the Williamite style is its delicate articulation and its modest scale, which always hints at domesticity of a kind that is omnipresent in the art of Holland in its golden age.

The parterre here is a miniature *parterre à l'angloise* inspired by those in the re-created baroque garden of William III at the palace of Het Loo, Apeldoorn, in the Netherlands, designed by the French émigré Daniel Marot and laid out from 1685 onwards. It is an area of closely clipped grass cut into a pattern, set against coloured gravel and surrounded by a ribbon of box-edged beds, known as the *plate-bande*, containing seasonal flowers. Such a garden calls for a handsome focal point: I would suggest a finial or urn in the late seventeenth-century style on a classical pedestal, which are now obtainable in reconstituted stone at a reasonable prices, or a reproduction statue in the baroque idiom. For those who would like to grow more flowers, it would be in period to have a flower garden as an alternative to the parterre. I have included a design (overleaf) based on a pattern in the 1721 edition of *Den Nederlandsten Hovenier*, which first appeared in 1669. This allows for a far richer and varied planting of a kind which can be seen today, for example, in the re-created parterre at Westbury-upon-Severn, Gloucestershire. I have also included a third alternative, which dispenses with flowers altogether and so would be the easiest to maintain, adapted from Leonard Meager's pattern book, *The English Gardener* (1670). A re-created garden of this type from the same pattern book can be seen at Little Moreton Hall, Congleton, Cheshire.

The canal garden owes its inspiration to the canal at Westbury, which has a handsome two-storey summerhouse in the Wren manner standing at its head and reflected in its waters (see page 45). This is replaced here by a pavilion copied from a design in *Den Nederlandsten Hovenier* and painted green-blue. The canal need only be shallow as its purpose is to reflect the sky and the pavilion in its waters. Its length is emphasized by a series of strong vertical accents from clipped yews interspersed with standard guelder roses. A

The *plate-bande* that surrounds the parterre can be filled with a wide range of plants (see page 147), but to convey the correct impression. they should be placed about 3ft (90cm) apart. Here honeysuckle wound tightly round a painted pole and a wigwam of sweetpeas rise above campanula, lychnis and hellebore. Another, simpler, solution would be to fill the bed with a single species, for example *Ruta graveolens* or *Santolina chamaecyparissus* – as in the illustration opposite.

crataegus hedge (which could be cut into deep swags) acts as a boundary. Apart from regular cutting of the grass and annual clipping of the topiary and hedge, this is not a labour-intensive garden, although no one should be tempted into making a canal without taking into account all the usual requirements of maintaining a water garden. In terms of initial construction costs this garden would not be cheap – and although the change of level is not essential, it adds to period authenticity; the effect, however, would be spectacular, even on a scale as small as this.

The grove is a revival of a delightful garden concept that has been lost over the centuries: this is a reduction of one at a house called Ackham which appears in one of the engravings in Knyff and Kip's *Britannia Illustrata* (1709). An arrangement of trees and hedges of varying heights, it makes an ideal model for a decorative orchard. The enclosing beech hedge adds the drama of changing colour in winter and autumn, as it turns from green to russet and caramel. If there was more space within the grove, add the roses and flowering shrubs which would have been included at that period.

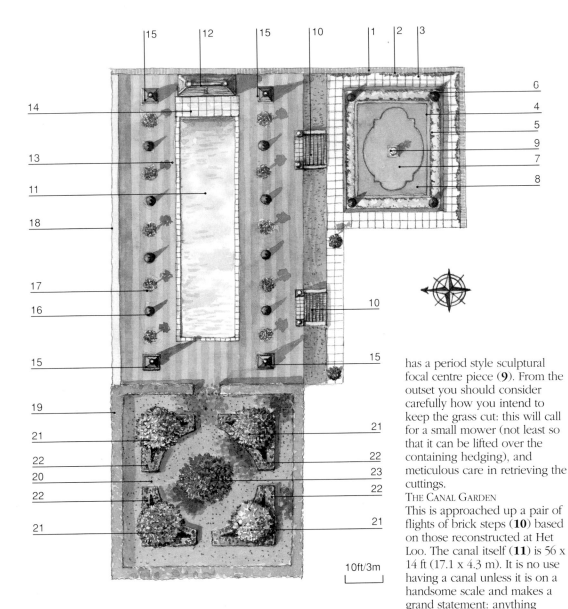

10ft/3m

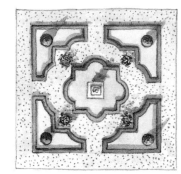

THE PARTERRE

The brick wall (**1**) provides the attractive possibility of growing espaliered fruit trees (**2**). A hedge of yew, hornbeam or holly would, of course, be an alternative. The parterre is surrounded by a path (**3**) of stone or slabs 4 ft (1.2 m) wide. The *plate-bande* or flower border is about 3 ft 6 in (1.1 m) wide and edged with box (**4**). It is filled with clipped santolina (**5**) and has yew cones (**6**), about 5 ft (1.5 m) high at the four corners. The level area of grass (**7**) is cut into a decorative pattern typical of the period and firmly held in place with a concealed plastic edging. It is set against red gravel, stone chippings or brick dust (**8**), and has a period style sculptural focal centre piece (**9**). From the outset you should consider carefully how you intend to keep the grass cut: this will call for a small mower (not least so that it can be lifted over the containing hedging), and meticulous care in retrieving the cuttings.

THE CANAL GARDEN

This is approached up a pair of flights of brick steps (**10**) based on those reconstructed at Het Loo. The canal itself (**11**) is 56 x 14 ft (17.1 x 4.3 m). It is no use having a canal unless it is on a handsome scale and makes a grand statement: anything smaller would resemble a surburban pond and is best avoided. It need not be deep, however, 3 ft (90 cm) being sufficient. The lining should be painted black to emphasize the water's reflective qualities and maximize its role as a mirror for the sky and the pavilion at the far end (**12**). This simple wooden construction is painted green-blue and could be covered in honeysuckle. The canal has a stone edging (**13**), and a terrace (**14**) designed to be spacious enough for a formal arrangement of plants in containers in the summer. On each side of the canal is a procession of trained shrubs, a feature typical of Dutch canal gardens of the period. Here there are four large yew obelisks (**15**) about 10 ft (3 m) high which act as anchors, eight yew cones (**16**) about 6 ft (1.8 m) high – which match those in the parterre – and ten guelder roses (*Viburnum opulus* 'Roseum') trained as standards (**17**). These bear large frothy white flowerheads in late spring or early summer and red fruits in autumn. Standard honeysuckles (*Lonicera sempervirens*) would be another possibility. A really lavish alternative to the four huge yew obelisks would be life-size statues of the four seasons on pedestals in the Vincenza style, or other statues in the baroque idiom. A hedge of *Crataegus*

ABOVE A simple flower garden would be a valid alternative to a turf parterre. Here box cones rise from box-edged beds that could be filled with a succession of seasonal period flowers.

LEFT A parterre design of 1703-12 by Daniel Marot, with cut turf surrounded by a *plate-bande* which is punctuated by topiary sentinels. The *plate-bande* would have been edged with box.
RIGHT Two designs for wooden obelisks from Jan van der Groen's *Den Nederlandtsen Hovenier* (1669). These would have been painted and used as supports for climbing plants.
BELOW A Dutch garden of *c.*1660-70. The small villa looks down onto a formal garden with two fountains surrounded by grass and clipped shrubs in containers. A vista to a hedge forms an exedra before which stands a white trellis obelisk flanked by topiary cake-stands. Other box-edged beds contain shrubs and through the pretty white fencing to the right there is an orchard.

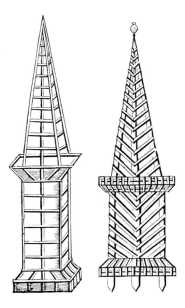

monogyna (**18**) runs along the north boundary.

THE GROVE

The containing hedge (**19**) of beech (*Fagus sylvatica*) or hornbeam (*Carpinus betulus*) will provide a change of colour in autumn and winter. Within this lies a patch of rough cut grass (**20**) and a simple planting of two pairs of dwarf rootstock apple or pear trees (**21**), each surrounded by a low hedge (**22**) of firethorn (*Pyracantha coccinea*), a hardy evergreen which bears white flowers in late spring or early summer and bright orange berries in autumn. In the centre is a specimen tree (**23**), chosen to act as a focal point to close the vista from the pavilion. Here it is a cherry plum (*Prunus cerasifera*) but it could be any handsome tree of the period, taking into consideration its shape, leaf form and colour, fruit and flowers. I have suggested a wooden seat to encompass its bole, which should be painted the same colour as the pavilion.

AN EARLY NEW ENGLAND GARDEN

The enchanting quality of this re-creation of a formal garden of pre-revolutionary America springs from the utter modesty and lack of pretension, and the strong sense of order that were the hallmarks of the style of the age. Colonial Williamsburg was the capital of Virginia from 1699 to 1781 and, thanks to the massive restoration project undertaken from 1926, it is now filled with gardens re-created in the Anglo-Dutch formal style which prevailed until the close of the eighteenth century. As it was decreed that the citizens' gardens were to be on average an acre (0.4 hectares) in size, these re-creations are a treasure trove of ideas for small gardens of the period, unequalled anywhere else. The amount of ornamental gardening was necessarily small, and usually confined to the approach to the house, as the majority of the land was given over to vegetables and herbs for the household and to the necessary outbuildings. In their simple adaptation of the best elements of the Anglo-Dutch tradition in gardening, and with their picket fences, patterned brick paths and delightful use of clipped evergreens, these gardens speak clearly of their own time while simultaneously suggesting a delightful formula for today's gardens.

This design includes a front garden and a potager, and assumes a framework of mature trees *outside* its confines to set it off to advantage in terms of scale, as its delicate, almost toy-like, dimensions form a contrast to the substantial boles and spreading branches of the trees. If your site does not include such features I would advise the introduction of at least one sizeable tree, such as an *Acer pensylvanicum* or *A. griseum*, at the expense of space in the potager.

The front garden is loosely inspired by the Bryan garden at Williamsburg. Enclosed by a simple picket fence, it relies heavily on brick paths and evergreens (in Virginia, yew and box were replaced by *Ilex vomitoria*, the native yaupon) and would require little maintenance. The spaces within the box-edged beds could be filled with flowers of the period or, for a virtually maintenance-free garden, you could fill them with groundcover plants such as lamium, epimedium, iberis or vinca.

The potager is a mélange of Williamsburg motifs: gravel paths, brick-edged beds, low espaliered apple trees and a handsome evergreen topiary centrepiece. A comfortable wooden seat is placed at one end of the main vista. These colonial gardens contained a proliferation of outbuildings, so instead of being hidden away the garden shed should be incorporated as part of the visual design, perhaps closing the vista through the cherry laurel hedge.

The garden lies on an irregular corner site, with the house to one side and facing south-west. In front of the house is an almost square garden 44 x 40 ft (13.4 x 12.2 m) and to one side is a vegetable garden, 56ft (17.1 m) on its longest side and with a truncated curve following the line of the street on the other side. It is assumed that there is more space to the north-east.

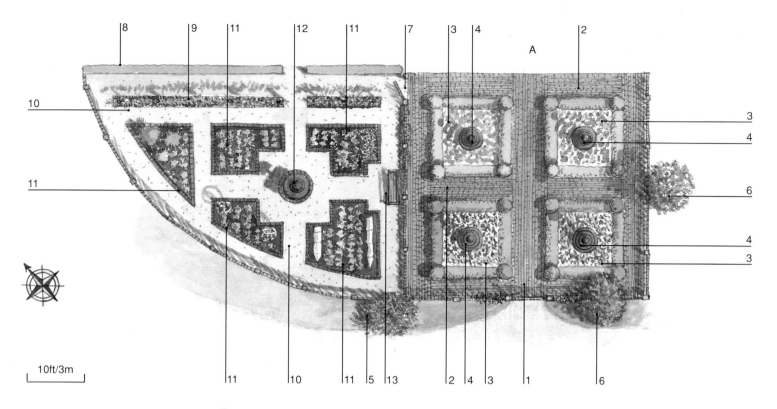

10ft/3m

Simple wooden seats such as this feature in many of the re-created gardens in Williamsburg. Here it is surrounded by a colourful cacophony of flowers: a trumpet vine, nasturtiums and poppies. As the proximity of sweet smelling plants would add to the pleasure of sitting down, you might include honeysuckle or roses.

THE FRONT GARDEN

A brick path (**1**), 6 ft (1.8 m) wide, leads from a gate in the simple picket fence to the front door of the house (**A**). Other paths (**2**), which are 4 ft (1.2 m) wide, divide and surround the area. The four beds (**3**), each 14 ft (4.3 m) square, are contained by box hedges, clipped loosely to make a curved silhouette and rising to domes at the corners. In the centre of each bed is a topiary cake-stand (**4**) of yaupon (*Ilex vomitoria*) or, if the climate does not allow this, yew (*Taxus baccata*). The beds can be filled with period flowers (see page 148); here they are block-planted with violas but it would be more interesting, if more time-consuming as well, to include a mixture of perennials, biennials and annuals. At the time any flowering plant that could be obtained would have

been planted and nurtured. Climbers such as honeysuckles and roses are growing along the boundary fences, which could also be underplanted with self-seeding annuals such as valerian, aquilegia, nigella, nepeta and poppies. Beyond the fence stands a lilac tree (**5**), and two *Cornus mas* (**6**). A Judas tree (*Cercis canadensis*) or a *Robinia pseudoacacia* would also give you attractive spring blossom.

THE POTAGER

The vegetable garden, entered by a picket gate (**7**) from the front garden, is enclosed on the north-east side by a hedge of cherry laurel (*Prunus laurocerasus*) (**8**). A row of low espaliered apple trees (**9**) runs parallel to the hedge; a row of currant bushes would be as authentic. They are underplanted with forget-me-nots, which could be replaced

ABOVE This alternative layout for the front garden is closely based on the Powell-Waller House garden in Williamsburg. A circular brick path is crossed by two transverse paths – one terminated by two seats – allowing for eight box-edged flowerbeds. The outer four spandrel beds have topiary cones to add height to the design.

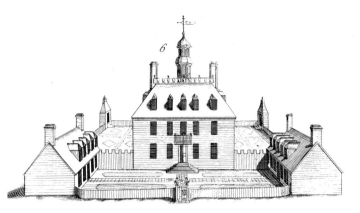

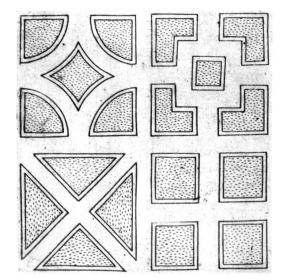

with marigolds or nasturtiums later in the year. The main area is gravelled (**10**) and divided into geometrical beds, edged in brick (**11**) and slightly raised, for vegetables and herbs. The range of vegetables grown at the time was limited but included such basic staples as onions, potatoes, spinach, cauliflower and cabbage, squash, pumpkin, artichokes, garlic, asparagus, carrots, beans, peas and lettuce. You will probably want to augment the list with more exotic vegetables which are available today. The list of contemporary herbs, however is very wide – herbs were used for medicinal as well as culinary use – and many are as decorative as they are useful. In the centre is a striking yew cut into a bold topiary shape (**12**). The bench (**13**) is painted the same grey-white as the picket fence.

LEFT The Governor's Mansion, Williamsburg, Virginia, about 1740. A rare view of an American colonial garden, a walled enclosure with summerhouses at the corners and laid out as a chequerboard of beds in the European style of a century earlier, evidence of both the time-lag and of conservatism in taste.

ABOVE Fellows' gardens at Jesus College, Oxford, 1675. The universities in England were conservative and here, too, the gardens are early seventeenth century in design: separate squares with geometric beds edged with box. This style of garden was to persist in New England even after the Declaration of Independence, although by then it had taken on a life of its own.
ABOVE LEFT Patterns for beds in Leonard Meager's *The English Gardener* (1670) which went through eleven editions and would have been a typical handbook for garden-making in the colonies.
LEFT The title page of Meager's *The New Art of Gardening* (1697) which would have been used in New England. It shows many ingredients typical of the colonial style, especially the division of space into strong geometric shapes.

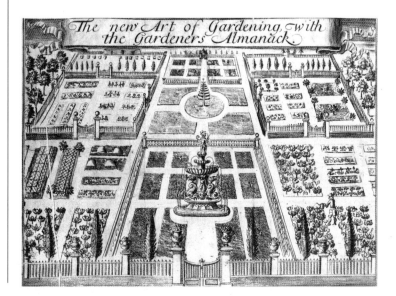

Age of Elegance

1720~1820

*I*f the sixteenth century belonged to Italy and the seventeenth century to France, the eighteenth century witnessed the triumph of England in the spread across Europe and eventually into the New World of the landscape style. This was a far greater revolution in gardening terms than those which preceded it, demanding as it did the sweeping away of horticultural masterpieces whose loss we now mourn, along with the gardening skills that created t hem. Its origins lay in the writings and ideas of the late seventeenth century, for instance in Sir William Temple's (1628-99) descriptions of Chinese gardens,

The layout of this large English town garden in Bristol is typical of the last years of the eighteenth century in its informal gardenesque style. Several views of it were recorded by a member of the Pole family in about 1806, but the garden was made at least a decade earlier. Serpentine gravel paths link outbuildings, including a soil sterilizing room, and provide walks for the purpose of exercise. Flowerbeds in different shapes are cut into the turf, and trees are placed asymmetrically, as is the one ornament, a classical urn.

whose perfection lay in their *sharawadgi*, or irregularity, and in the philosopher Earl of Shaftesbury's (1671-1713) praise of the 'horrid graces of the Wilderness'. They and others were reflecting a new visual perception of the garden, springing from an associational response involving both the intellect and the emotions.

The basic concern of all garden design henceforth was no longer to be the imposition of order on a given site, but rather the expression of the nature of the place itself, the *genius loci*. Such changes in the role of the garden began to be explored by the poet Alexander Pope (1688-1744), whose garden at Twickenham became a place of pilgrimage. There formality was banished in favour of creating a series of pictures inspired by painters such as Claude Lorraine, evoking states of mind and moods in visitors by means of planting, garden buildings and ornaments. William Kent (1685-1748), the architect and painter, was to take this revolution forward in a whole series of

gardens which he designed in the 1720s and 30s. He headed a series of mighty figures, foremost among them being Lancelot 'Capability' Brown (1716-83) and Humphry Repton (1752-1818), who take us through into the next century. The style itself, with variations, crossed the Channel to France, where *le jardin anglo-chinois* became fashionable in the two decades preceding the French Revolution, and to Germany during the same period. And Thomas Jefferson, who had visited the great English exemplars, distilled their inspiration into his famous garden at Monticello.

No period in the history of gardening is so intellectually complex, for the landscape style went through several phases. But for those wishing to create a small period garden there is a larger and more insuperable barrier, for the landscape style is one which cannot be exploited satisfactorily on very small sites. These gardens were simply enormous, concerned with orchestrating vast parks around country houses and princely

LEFT Created in the 1930s, this eighteenth-century-style flower garden in Charleston, South Carolina, shows how the formal tradition continued in America. The usual arrangement of symmetrical beds are edged with clipped box and brick set into gravel. The pretty springtime planting of modern pink tulips with a camellia as a focal point is anachronistic: the latter only appeared in the gardens of the wealthy in the first half of the nineteenth century, while the planting of tulips in blocks was a Victorian idea.

RIGHT Restored according to the results of archaeological research in 1990, this town garden in Bath, Avon, has been laid out as it would have appeared in about 1775, though it remained basically unchanged until 1836. The design was strictly formal, and the stone paths flanking the box-edged flowerbeds beneath the walls were planned to give the illusion from the house that the garden was rectangular instead of trapezoidal. The middle part was gravelled and contained three flowerbeds, a central oval one, flanked by two smaller circular ones. Originally the gravelled area would also have been enlivened by plants in containers. The trellis screen and seat are convincing additions to what is otherwise a rare instance of a scrupulously documented restoration.

LEFT An American Colonial flower garden of about 1760, re-created in the grounds of the Pennsylvania Horticultural Society, Philadelphia, in 1966, demonstrates the continuing strength of the formal tradition in America and the way in which the planting was adapted to native species, in this instance with topiary of native junipers. The beds are set off by stone edging and gravel walks, and contain an anachronistic display of nineteenth-century bedding-out plants.

The orange tree garden at Chiswick House, London, was laid out as part of the 3rd Earl of Burlington's gardens by William Kent and Charles Bridgeman in about 1715-25 and restored in the 1980s. With its asymmetrical design, crossed by vistas, the garden was one of the flagships of the new natural style. The orange tree garden itself was designed by Kent as an Italianate amphitheatre of turf steps, dotted in summer with orange trees in tubs (three times the number seen here).

The classical temple and the obelisk reflected in the still waters of the pool, together with surrounding trees, capture the painterly quality which the pioneers of the style sought to achieve: a vision of a pastoral arcadia as depicted in the much admired canvases of Claude Lorraine.

seats. They involved the making of large artificial lakes, woodlands, copses, cascades, waterfalls, glades and idealized farmland, not to mention buildings ranging from ruined castles to watermills and from pagodas to hermitages. There are, of course, lessons to be learned from them which can be useful in small spaces: a single statue placed in a well-planted glade, or the use of almost any form of building to enhance the appearance of a garden. But here for the first time we are dealing with a garden style which has relevance in this century only for town-planners or landscape architects.

But as the designs in this section demonstrate, small gardens did exist, and it is to those that we must turn, firstly to trace the survival of the flower garden into the Victorian period, and secondly to hail the arrival of the small town garden. In each case there is a depressingly small trickle of visual information in comparison with the plethora of evidence, both actual and graphic, which plots the landscape story. The first line of descent, termed the gardenesque, leads us directly to the first great popularizer of the small garden, John Claudius Loudon (1783-1843). In spite of the triumph of the landscape style, the eighteenth century in England witnessed an intense interest in flowers which only escalated as the century progressed and voyages of discovery, such as Captain Cook's, brought back their treasures. Already in the 1730s there were gardens which were dedicated to the cultivation of flowers, not in the regimented manner of the baroque age but in a quite different style, responding to the newfangled vogue for *sharawadgi*. In the 1730s Richard, or Dickie, Bateman planted what must have been one of the earliest asymmetrical flower gardens, at Grove House, Windsor, a fenced enclosure away from the house with a wooden arbour on a small mount surrounded by flowerbeds in different shapes scattered over the turf. Bateman was a friend of Joseph Spence (1699-1768), Professor of Poetry at Oxford, a prolific designer for his friends of small gardens in the gardenesque style, most of which were concerned with flowers.

Spence was a great influence on Sir William Chambers (1723-96) who at Kew laid out a formal flower garden around a central pond for Princess Augusta between 1757 and 1763. But the real milestone occurred in 1771, when the poet William Mason (1725-97) designed the famous flower garden at Nuneham Courtenay for Lord Harcourt. Here, away from the park, he created an enclosure crossed by winding paths and enclosed by trees and shrubs, which acted as a foil to the luscious display of flowers, planted in descending heights, in

LEFT The summerhouse was a standard ingredient in almost all eighteenth-century American gardens. This one, at Gunston Hall, Virginia, is an appealing re-creation of such a building. The gardens that it stands in were originally designed in the 1750s by George Mason, (whose library was filled with French and English garden books of the previous century), and were restored shortly after 1913, unfortunately before the era of accurate garden history research.

RIGHT ABOVE The gardens at Rousham House, Oxfordshire, laid out in the 1720s and 30s, were William Kent's masterpiece *genius loci*. Here a statue of Pan, the pagan god of the woodlands, gives identity to a sylvan glade and makes a feature that could be copied on a much smaller scale.

RIGHT BELOW A serpentine wall of about 1819, as designed by Thomas Jefferson for the gardens of the University of Virginia, begun in 1817, and restored from 1948 to 1951. Serpentine walls, a feature of some English kitchen gardens from the middle of the eighteenth century, were designed to run from east to west, in order to reflect maximum sunlight on the trees planted against them, and hence hasten the ripening of the fruit.

asymmetrical beds set into turf. This new naturalistic arrangement of the flower garden owed a great deal to the influence of the French philosopher, Jean-Jacques Rousseau, and his descriptions of the disposition of flowers in *La Nouvelle Héloïse* (1761). All these developments combined to yield the ingredients for the flower gardens Repton was to create in the early nineteenth century, which in turn heralded the gardens of the Victorian age.

Flower gardens were by their nature small, and it is to them that we must look for inspiration for today's small gardens. By 1800 their format was determined. They could either be formal, as typified by Kew, or irregular, as exemplified by Nuneham Courtenay. The formal element owed much to the French, and there was already a revival of *ancien régime* formality in the

aftermath of the Napoleonic wars. In the newly formed United States the formal tradition was never broken, and continued on through the revolutionary period into the new century.

Gardening still remained largely the prerogative of the rich, and it was they who, at the beginning of the nineteenth century in search of a new informality of life and closer commune with the world of nature, 'discovered' the delights of small-scale living. While the rural poor lived in direst poverty, the aristocracy and gentry built *cottages ornés*, in both the classical and the Gothick style, retreats suitable for 'men of study, science or leisure'. Adorned with verandahs, and climbing plants, they were surrounded by small flower gardens of direct eighteenth-century descent. These had lawns with winding walks and shrubberies, and flowerbeds cut into the

turf close to the main living room so that the flowers could be enjoyed to the full while their scent wafted inside.

Developing in parallel with *cottages ornés* were town gardens, small rectangular tongues of land at the back of the terraces and squares of houses which sprang up in London and Bath during the century. J.C. Loudon described their value for the owner '[he] should surround his plot with an oval path, that he may walk on without end and without any sensible change in the position of his body'. The most important feature of all these gardens was clearly their gravelled walks. As these houses were usually used only seasonally, the design of the gardens rarely rose above a central area of green turf and a surrounding border of trees and shrubs. These had to contend with heavy air pollution caused by the smoke from coal fires, which explains the huge popularity of container plants for both the house and the garden. It was only as the century progressed that proper town gardens developed, with built structures to act as eye-catchers, flowerbeds and other delights.

More important than this in the long term, perhaps, was the plant dialogue with America which was to transform the flower garden. The key figure in this story was the Quaker John Bartram (1699-1777) who sent on subscription to British gardeners an annual box of seeds of about a hundred different species. Among those were the first American rhododendrons and magnolias and a large number of aster and phlox species. This influx was complemented by a burgeoning commercial nursery industry, dedicated to propagating plants and making them available to an ever widening public. By the close of the eighteenth century all the ingredients were in place for a vast expansion in garden-making.

By 1820 the long reign of nature was reaching its end, to be followed by the high artifice of the nineteenth century. Much more important were the huge social changes in the wake of the French Revolution, which meant that prosperity began to spread over a much broader social spectrum, and pleasure gardening gradually ceased to be the prerogative of a small section of society. The eighteenth century, with its rich mercantile classes, saw the beginnings of a new phenomenon, the consumer society. Those aspiring classes increasingly had both the leisure and the means to want to create gardens, drawing on what they saw in the great aristocratic parks. The result was to be the suburban villa, and the emergence for the first time of a whole section of book and magazine publishing devoted to what we recognize today as the small garden.

A GEORGIAN TOWN GARDEN

Eighteenth-century town gardens succeeded in combining a number of alfresco delights in a very small space. This garden includes gravel walks, places to sit, decorative architecture and a full seasonal planting that includes small trees, shrubs, flowers, climbers and culinary herbs. It was a style of garden that evolved to suit perfectly those small narrow tongues of land jutting out at the back of terraced houses which were the invention of the early eighteenth century.

The design of these gardens was always formal. Those belonging to the very rich would have been paved in stone, contained by brick walls and equipped with an architectural eyecatcher, an obelisk or arch perhaps, to close the vista. The majority would have been more modest, surrounded by wooden fences about 5 ft (1.5 m) high and laid out in geometrical designs with gravel walks taking the place generally occupied by lawns today. Great importance was attached to walks: daily walking was held in high esteem for its benefits to health, and was one of the few forms of exercise deemed acceptable for ladies. Gravel was useful not only because it was inexpensive, but also because it could be raked over to conceal the discoloration by the appalling levels of air pollution caused by the coal fires.

A great number of plans of eighteenth-century town gardens survive in maps of the period. From these it is clear that the disposition of space within the gardens tended to follow similar general lines: a series of beds in the centre would be surrounded by a wide gravel walk, which in turn would be edged by perimeter beds beneath the fence or walls. Pergolas or summerhouses were fairly common, but just as frequently the only garden building would be the earth closet. The planting, to judge from the very few instances in which we know the details of it, was necessarily limited to trees and plants which were able to survive in the soot-laden atmosphere. Trees must have been rigorously pruned in order to contain them within such tiny spaces, and replaced once they had outgrown the area. Great emphasis was laid on fruit trees and on sweet-smelling flowers and climbers.

The design here is drawn from ones by the Reverend Joseph Spence (1699-1768), Professor of Poetry at Oxford and an amateur garden designer (who incidentally came to an unfortunate end in his ornamental canal). It combines elements from Spence's plan for a house in Bond Street in 1743 and another for Lady Falmouth's garden the following year. The former was only 50 x 20 ft (15.2 x 6.1 m) and the latter 50 x 40 ft (15.2 x 12.2 m), yet within these confined boundaries Spence included vines, elms, laburnums, almonds, lilacs and an assortment of flowers. He recommended training creepers up the back of the house in order to extend the feeling of the garden, and adding flowers in containers during the summer months: on windowsills, grouped along the railings, arranged on wooden display benches like auricula stands, or simply dotted at intervals along the gravel walks. The buildings – the central pavilion and Gothick arbour – are inspired by those seen in the watercolours of Thomas Robins (1716-70).

A formal eighteenth-century flower garden such as this would not be a daunting prospect in terms either of work or of cost. In addition, we would today be able to choose from a far wider range of period plants, thanks to the post-war legislation on clean air. This type of garden remained essentially unchanged until the very close of the eighteenth century, when at last the effects of the landscape revolution filtered down to the domestic level, and formality was abandoned in favour of a central lawn surrounded by shrubberies and a serpentine path.

The walls are enlivened with espaliered fruit trees trained onto a wooden frame. The narrow bed held in by boards allows just enough room for two tiers of flowers: here *Iris* 'Florentina', *germanica*, *pallida* and *variegata* have lower-growing flowers such as primulas and violas at their feet. A greater variety of period flowers could be grown today than would have survived in the soot-polluted atmosphere of the eighteenth century.

This is a tiny back garden, only 50 x 20 ft (15.2 x 6.1 m), designed for an enclosed, rectangular urban space typical of the eighteenth century. The back of the house faces north

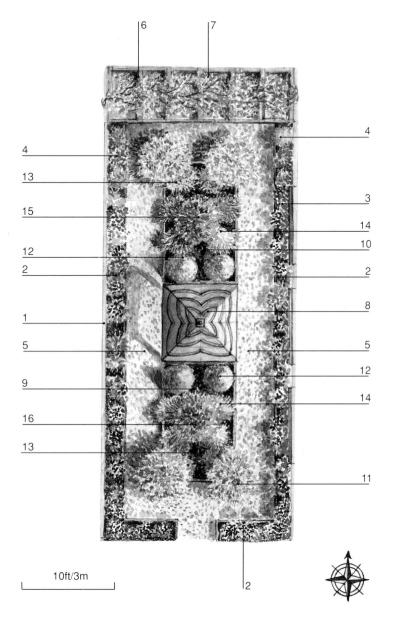

10ft/3m

beds also give space for spot-planting of period flowers such as known varieties of iris – 'Florentina', *germanica, pallida* and *variegata* – along with lavender, dianthus and viola (see page 148). At the northern end I have suggested planting a group of culinary herbs such as rosemary and sage (**4**).The gravel walks (**5**) are only some 4 ft (1.2 m) wide; at the time it would have been preferred for them to be 6 or even 8 ft (1.8 or 2.4 m) wide. They may be paved with stone if you prefer, but gravel is undoubtedly the most authentic material, and is easy to maintain if laid to a good depth (about a foot or 30 cm). At the north end of the garden is a simple pergola (**6**), faced with a Gothick fret painted off-white. A vine is trained over it for summer shade and autumn colour. The pergola stands on a slightly raised paved area and has a comfortable wooden seat (**7**), preferably in the Gothick style if you can find or adapt one. The central pavilion (**8**) in the Chinese taste then so fashionable is inspired by the work of Thomas Robins, whose watercolours depict a bewildering array of pavilions and gazebos in exotic and fanciful styles. At the time no one would have thought twice about placing two buildings in such eclectic styles in close proximity to each other in a garden. The woodwork is painted the same off-white as the pergola, and the building is surmounted by a gilded finial. Similar summerhouses are still manufactured commercially, though the roofs will now be of fibreglass. Garden furniture in the Chippendale Chinese manner, like the table and

chairs beneath it, is certainly available. Honeysuckle (*Lonicera* × *italica*) twines up two of the supporting pillars. The two central beds (**9** and **10**), again boarded in, are only 13 x 8 ft (3.9 x 2.4 m) and contain a simple symmetrical planting that includes evergreens, plants with grey foliage and flowering trees. Two pairs of *Laburnum anagyroides* (**11**), hung with glorious yellow racemes in spring, but less interesting for the rest of the year, stand as sentinels at the corners. Almonds, Spence's great favourite, would be another possibility, with their pretty pale pink blossom; or Judas trees; or even false acacias for their feathery foliage. Whichever trees you choose, they will have to be pruned to contain them within the space, and will eventually need replacing. The mirror-image planting of the beds continues with two pairs *of Ilex aquifolium* (**12**), two pairs of *Phlomis fruticosa* (**13**) and four pairs of *Lavandula angustifolia* (**14**). In addition there are two roses: *Rosa* × *damascena versicolor* (**15**) and *Rosa* × *centifolia* 'Muscosa' (**16**). The spaces in between can be spot-planted with period flowers. The back of the house, following Spence's prescription, would have had a *Clematis viticella* and a *Jasminum officinale* trained up it. And do not forget to add flowers in containers in summer. The colour scheme here, of grey, yellow, pink and green, can be varied. Consideration would have been given to the height of the flowers, rising to the centre. As the century went on, the number of varieties expanded and the planting became denser.

Below the enclosing wall or fence (**1**) are narrow beds (**2**), each 2 ft (60 cm) wide, which border the south, east and west sides. They are boarded in and hence slightly raised, and where aspect allows contain espaliered fruit trees on wooden trellis panels (**3**) painted green. The choice of fruit can be varied according to individual taste

and aspect. If you are ambitious, greater decorative interest could be gained by employing other forms of training – fan or palmette would both be correct for the period. If, however, you want to reduce your workload in the garden, you could grow silver and gold variegated ivies up the walls instead of the fruit trees. The

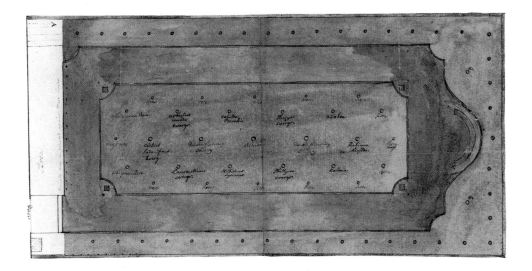

LEFT A design for a town garden of 25 x 53 ft (7.6 x 16.1 m) of 1791. In the centre is a box-edged bed contained by a wide gravel walk; this is surrounded by a box-edged herbaceous border which is backed by a dense clipped hedge of poplar. The central bed has a rose border for fragrance and is filled with flowering deciduous and evergreen shrubs and trees. Near the house is a terrace with walls and rails smothered in currants, privet, holly, laurel, honeysuckle, ivy and clematis. At the end of the garden is a seat within an arbour, also covered in climbers.

ABOVE This summerhouse from Paul Decker's *Gothic Architecture Restored and Improved...* (1759) is a typical instance of a whimsical wooden garden building from a pattern book. It could be copied and adapted by a local carpenter for a particular site.

LEFT The vista in a town garden belonging to a doctor, which was laid out in Gloucestershire in the 1740s, includes a proliferation of fanciful wooden decoration and the use of trees and shrubs in containers. Even in a space as small as this, evergreen architecture can form 'rooms' and vistas.

AN EARLY LANDSCAPE GARDEN

This garden looks both to the past and future. It combines the principles of the formal gardening of the previous century – based on the long avenue as the main axis, with a foretaste of the revolutionary landscape style to come – in the serpentine walk. The mix of tradition and novelty, of straight lines and twists and turns, is especially appealing in that it can be adapted to a site of virtually any shape or contour.

The ultimate source for this design is the poet Alexander Pope's famous garden beside the Thames at Twickenham, regarded as the forerunner of the English landscape style, which he started in 1719 and continued working on for the next twenty-five years. Within a rectangular framework covering some 5 acres (2 hectares), he set out to unite gardening and the visual arts, deploying plants to create 'landscape pictures' conceived for the first time directly in terms of painting. As Horace Walpole noted, 'it was a singular effort of art and taste to compress so much variety and scenery' into so modest a space. Rejecting the symmetry and regularity of the late baroque garden, Pope also banished such artful contrivances as parterres and topiary. His friend and contemporary William Kent was to develop the same ideas, albeit with a heavier debt to Italian prototypes, in the country estates of the aristocracy.

Pope's garden, though small by eighteenth-century standards, was none the less large by ours. Fortunately its principles were appropriated by his friend Joseph Spence, who in 1736 made a plan along similar lines for his own garden, and that design is the more direct inspiration for my own. Spence's design is more backward-looking than Pope's, for it retains the idea of using a formal vista as its main feature. In my plan, in essence, we see garden design at the crossroads: the meandering walks and greensward look forward to the work of Lancelot 'Capability' Brown, while the formal avenue and clipped hedges look backward to the age of George London and Henry Wise. Elements of formality would also originally have been retained in a quite separate flower garden. Here I have suggested incorporating flowers as part of the formality of the central vista. If you wish to take your garden forward in date while at the same time reducing maintenance you could dispense with all the clipped hedges, which Pope would certainly have condemned. In my view, however, they help to articulate and lend structure to a small area which might otherwise seem rather incoherent.

Next to the house a generous lawn (Pope's 'bowling green') gives space for twentieth-century family needs, overlooked by

A summer view, framed by two *Cupressus sempervirens*, from the long walk across the shrubbery to the urn in the serpentine walk. The *plate-bande* in the foreground, held in by boards, is still planted in the manner of the pre-landscape style, with plants – here foxgloves, blue *Veronica longifolia* and meadow buttercup (*Ranunculus acris* 'Flore Pleno') – spaced well apart.

a seat in a yew niche. From here the eye is drawn down a grand vista lined with cypresses and closed by an urn, which could be replaced with a grander statement, perhaps a small classical temple or a rustic grotto set back into the surrounding shrubbery. The prospect from here back to the house would be equally impressive. The shrubbery is mainly evergreen, and the serpentine walk is articulated by a low hornbeam hedge which would turn russet in winter, and punctuated by a circular clearing. Walks like this, with the occasional seat or ornament in a little clearing, can be re-cast to suit virtually any shape or size of garden.

In today's terms this is not a high-maintenance garden, requiring only mowing, an annual cut of the hedges, a seasonal pruning of the shrubs, and the work involved in the narrow flower borders. Those who wish to cut the workload still further could dispense with the hedges and the flowerbeds. The few ornaments – easily available in reconstituted stone in authentic period styles – may entail a heavy initial outlay, but are essential to the success of the scheme.

The main avenue runs due east and the area covered is about 165 x 65 ft (51 x 19.8 m) and uneven in shape. A scheme such as this can accommodate any number of irregularities at the boundaries simply by extending the shrub planting. The land rises or falls slightly as it recedes from the house.

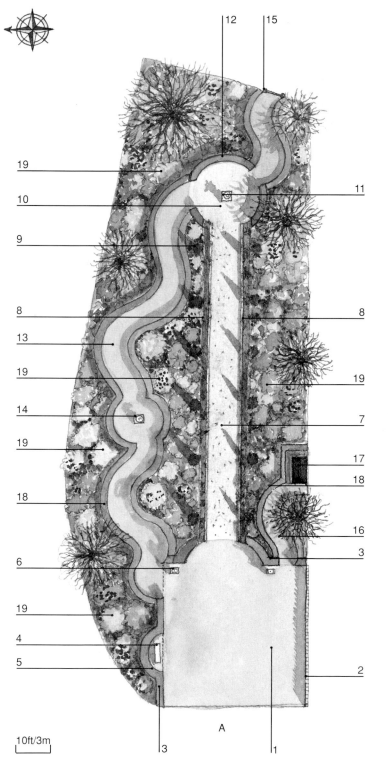

10ft/3m

The Lawn

The lawn (**1**) is 36 ft (11 m) square and bounded by the house (**A**) to the west, a wall or fence to the south (**2**), and yew hedges (**3**) 8 ft (2.4 m) high on the other two sides. A terrace could be added under the house, or used to replace the grass if preferred. If there is no boundary wall or fence the hedge could be extended along that side as well. On one side a stone bench (**4**) is set within an exedra (**5**), and a second, open, exedra frames the main walk and is flanked by two stone obelisks (**6**).

The Main Walk

The main walk (**7**) is 80 ft (24.3 m) long, 8 ft (2.4 m) wide and gravelled. It is flanked by narrow flowerbeds (**8**) retained by boards, which could accommodate a full range of period flowers planted in the *plate-bande* manner spanning the main flowering seasons (see the plant list on page 148). The beds are backed by an avenue of cypresses (*Cupressus sempervirens*) (**9**) inspired by the one which in Pope's garden led to the memorial to his mother. Here it leads to a gravel circus (**10**), 18 ft (5.5 m) in diameter, with a large urn (**11**) about 8 ft (2.4 m) high placed at the centre and contained by a clipped yew hedge (**12**). An alternative here would perhaps be to dispense with the urn and the backing hedge and to place a small classical temple set back into the shrubbery. Temples of the correct styles in reconstituted stone are available in several forms, but are not cheap.

The Serpentine Walks and Groves

The main meandering walk (**13**) forms a startling contrast to the straight central avenue. It is punctuated with another smaller circus (**14**) 12 ft (3.6 m) in diameter which has a different urn about 6 ft (1.8 m) high at the centre. The path leads eventually to a gate (**15**) at the far end of the garden. Another minor walk (**16**) leads to a garden shed (**17**). In Spence's design the serpentine walk is sanded, but these could equally well be gravelled. I have introduced low hornbeam (*Carpinus betulus*) containing hedges (**18**), about 3 ft 6 in (1.1 m) high, a feature typical of the wildernesses and groves of earlier formal gardens. This could be dispensed with, though it does help to give a strong structure to what could easily become an untidy thoroughfare. The path winds through a shrubbery (**19**) planted in the main with evergreens, with taller bushes such as common laurel being placed as screening at the boundaries. The planting in these groves was unbelievably dense: elms, chestnuts and other substantial trees were placed a mere 3 ft (90 cm) apart, with only 6 ft (1.8 m) between the rows. Here, as we are dealing with a small space, I would suggest filling it with the sort of shrubs and small trees, like euonymus, rhamnus, hazel and *Cornus mas*, that were used in the making of *bosquets* and wildernesses of the seventeenth century and are still easily obtainable today. The best way is to work out a framework of evergreens and then add a few deciduous shrubs, such as lilac or philadelphus, for colour and scent. For more planting interest, work tall flowers such as martagon lilies, *Campanula latifolia* and foxgloves into the margins.

LEFT Part of the garden of Claremont, *c*.1742-45, William Kent's masterpiece: an enticing downhill walk to young trees arranged in groups, which is controlled by evergreen hedges clipped into obelisks and bays to accomodate benches. Kent composed his garden pictures using a mixture of the new asymmetrical informality and formal elements from the previous century.

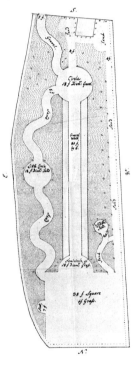

ABOVE Two large handsome garden urns designed by William Kent for Alexander Pope, *c*.1735. Both are available today in reconstituted stone, as are the plinths; together they are approximately 8-9 ft (2.4-2.7 m) high.

ABOVE The ground-plan by Joseph Spence for a garden at Birchanger in Surrey, upon which my design is based. The original plan covered an area of only 168 x 52 ft (51.2 x 15.8 m).
LEFT The wilderness at Trinity College, Oxford, *c*.1720, made up of clipped hedges containing densely-planted shrubs probably planted thirty years earlier, would have been old-fashioned by the 1720s. If it had been commissioned in 1720, the ground-plan would have been asymmetrical and meandering.

A NEW WORLD FLOWER GARDEN

American flower gardens of the late eighteenth century took on a life of their own, producing a style which has extraordinary appeal to us today. The formal tradition, deriving from seventeenth-century Europe, continued to remain vigorous since most of colonial America had neither the means nor the inclination to imitate the complex grandeur of the landscape movement. But as the century progressed, it saw the art of gardening flourish and, after 1776, the newly independent nation establish its own horticultural conventions. While flower gardens retained a geometric structure, they managed to achieve a new formality of the most delightfully loose kind. Domestic in scale, they display those qualities of modesty and simplicity which contemporary Europeans might have considered peripheral and provincial but which are very much in tune with today's lifestyle. Their small size and moderate maintenance requirements – the flower garden was after all traditionally the domain of the lady of the house, who would certainly not have been above working in it herself – mean that they are also both feasible and practical for twentieth-century gardeners.

The design is adapted from one to be found among the Skipwith papers at the College of William and Mary at Williamsburg, Virginia. These papers include two designs for, or records of, flower gardens which (although they are copies made later in the century) are among a collection of horticultural papers datable to the years 1785 to 1805. Sir Peyton Skipwith, having married for a second time in 1788, brought his new wife with him to the United States, where at Prestwold, Mecklenburg County, he built a fine new house. Jean, Lady Skipwith, meanwhile supervised the laying out of the gardens. She was a passionate gardener, as is revealed by the long lists of plants among her papers. One headed 'shrubs to be got when I can', bears witness to the predatory nature of a truly dedicated gardener, and another gives an inventory of her stock, including 'A tolerable collection of Roses, amongst which are a double and single yellow rose'. The great *Gardeners Dictionary*, compiled by Philip Miller and first published in 1731, was her bible and she seems also to have had access to William Curtis's *Botanical Magazine*, the earliest periodical devoted to gardening matters. Her designs displayed not only flowers from the Old World but also the native American species for which European gardeners were clamouring. The exchange of seeds and plants across the Atlantic was at fever pitch for most of the century.

One of the most striking aspects of these gardens is the absence of any pretentious built features or statuary. Their role was taken by boxwood and holly topiary, already long out of fashion in England by this time but still popular in America. Here it forms a handsome evergreen foil to a colourful display of herbaceous plants, with a strong emphasis on native species: rudbeckia, *Achillea millefolium*, gaillardia and *Galega officinalis*. Four box-edged spandrel beds meanwhile contain old roses, which give both height and early summer flowers in white and pink, a theme continued in the enclosing hedge of juniper and eglantine roses. The main display, however, is reserved for late summer and autumn, with a predominance of yellows giving unity to the colour scheme.

Although the main emphasis is on the later season, spring interest can of course be added by introducing bulbs among the rest of the planting, or you may even wish to give one of the beds over entirely to annuals in summer, thus allowing a spring display of tulips or hyacinths. The planting options in general are large; the roses, for example, could be replaced with clipped box cones, standard honeysuckles or a shrub such as Kalmia latifolia, a plant that was popular with both George Washington and Thomas Jefferson.

Any flower garden, by definition, cannot be anything other than an enthusiast's gardens, but the scale of this one is so diminutive that it ought not to be over demanding in terms of maintenance. Particular care should be taken to ensure that the beds are kept well enriched with compost. The perennials will need splitting up from time to time to keep them vigorous and to discourage them from spreading too much. The tall plants and climbers, such as sweet peas and morning glories, will need supporting, but this provides an opportunity to make pretty rustic features such as wigwams of stakes or beehives of twigs.

The eastern seaboard American flower gardens that we know about were always placed apart from the house and enclosed by hedges, which would more conventionally have been of box again or lilac. In the corners I have placed four small *Crataegus crus-galli* trees, which hold the whole composition together and signal its presence from afar. Such Old Virginian gardens, managing as they did to take on an Old World design framework, shake out any pomposity, and give it the relaxed elegance of the New, will amply repay any effort involved in re-creating one today, on whichever side of the Atlantic it may be.

The garden is 43 ft (10.4m) square and the trellis-work gazebo faces
north, providing shade in an otherwise open, sunny garden. These
gardens, traditionally away from the house, were always enclosed to
keep out unwanted livestock.

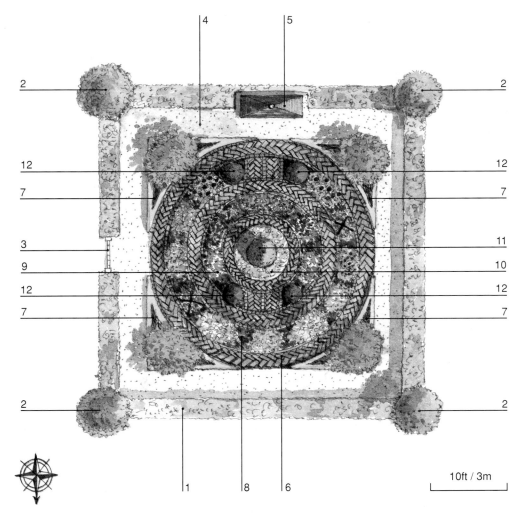

10ft / 3m

plants at the outset in order to give instant effect to the scheme. The box-edged spandrels (**7**) contain a symmetrical planting of roses from the Old World, but which were already well established in American gardens by this time: the white Jacobite Rose (*Rosa* 'Alba Maxima') and the pink Damask (*Rosa × damascena bifara*). An underplanting of snowdrops or other bulbs would add interest for spring. The planting structure of the two inner beds is made up of perennials, with yellow as the co-ordinating colour: rudbeckia, *Achillea millefolium, Helianthus annuus* and lemon hollyhocks. Other perennials such as goat's rue, gaillardia, dianthus and violas, as well as martagon lilies, fill the spaces in between, while wigwams of sweet peas or other flowering climbers would add height. Mignonette encircles the central box cone (**11**) lending the finishing touch to a display which at its late-summer height should be stunning. The planting can of course be varied, but I would always make sure that there was a single dominant colour. Silver-grey would be another possibility, using perennials such as lychnis, *Salvia officinalis*, dianthus and lavender. An alternative equally historical way to lay out the garden would be in the pattern of the Maltese cross, a favourite motif in the flower gardens of Old Virginia. As such gardens were often made up of multiples of the same pattern, if more space is available, simply lay out a repeat, perhaps dedicating it to varieties of a single species, for instance roses or peonies.

The garden is encompassed by a hedge (**1**) about 3 ft 6 in (1.1m) high, just tall enough to ensure protection from frost and wind, but not so high as to forbid the sun full play. I have chosen to use *Juniperus virginiana* and the wild eglantine rose, which would make for a pretty contrast and give a lovely effect when in flower, but the hedge could equally well be of box or lilac. In the corners are four small *Crataegus crus-galli* (**2**) which grow to a maximum height of 25 ft (7.6 m) but can be kept much smaller by pruning, and

which bear white flowers in spring and brilliant red fruits in autumn. A white-painted picket gate (**3**) let into the hedge gives access to the garden; an arch thrown over this and framed with honeysuckle would be a pretty addition. The flower beds are surrounded by a gravel path (**4**) 4 ft (1.2 m) wide, and an elegant summerhouse (**5**) is set into the hedge on the south side for shade. Three narrow circular brick paths (**6**), just 2 ft (60 cm) wide, create four spandrel beds edged with *Buxus sempervirens* 'Suffruticosa'(**7**); two concentric flower beds (**8** and **9**) which are

themselves only 3 ft (90 cm) wide; and a central round bed (**10**) which is about 8 ft (2.4m) in diameter. The beds are given year-round architectural structure and height by a central 5 ft (1.5 m) high cone of clipped tree box (*Buxus sempervirens*) (**11**) and four domes of holly or winter berry (*Ilex verticillata*) (**12**). *Ilex opaca*, or American holly would be alternatives. The topiary can be of any shape, but the central feature should be taller than the flowers around it if possible. As both box and holly are very slow-growing, it is worthwhile investing in large

BELOW A modern ground-plan of part of the upper garden at Mount Vernon, Washington D.C., laid out for George Washington in the 1780s. The narrow quarter-circle beds, divided by gravel paths, are edged with upturned bricks and filled with a mixture of shrubs, herbaceous plants and annuals.

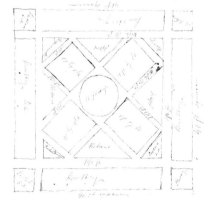

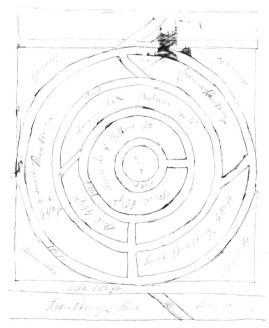

ABOVE and RIGHT These records or designs for flower gardens, now at Williamsburg, Virginia, were found among the papers of Jean, Lady Skipwith which can be dated to between 1785 and 1805. The outer beds contained shrubs, while the inner ones were planted with annuals and 'bulbous roots'. The paths were only 18 in (c.50 cm)wide.

ABOVE This design by William Kent, probably drawn up for Lady Burlington's flower garden at Chiswick House, Twickenham, Middlesex, in about 1730-3, shows how such gardens managed to survive the landscape garden era as small areas tucked away in the grounds and dedicated to the delight of flowers. Here a rustic temple is reflected in the still waters of a small circular pond, handy for watering; narrow semi-circular beds, still on the scale of the *plate-bande* of the previous century, contain the flowers; and a Negro servant adds to the display of container plants, an important element in eighteenth-century gardening.

A REGENCY FLOWER GARDEN

The elegance and sophistication of Jane Austen's England are epitomized in miniature in this garden. It combines architectural charm, rustic simplicity and a profusion of shrubs and flowers, all designed to be enjoyed from the shelter of a pretty trelliswork verandah, tree seat or Gothick arbour. This style of garden is as eminently suitable for cottages today as it was when it first appeared in the late eighteenth century when two related changes in the way people viewed their surroundings combined to produce the renaissance of the flower garden. Firstly, the upper classes discovered a taste for informality and the simple virtues of rural life, the most intrepid of them forsaking their draughty halls for whimsical and conveniently idealized pastiches of the hovels of the rural poor, dubbed *cottages ornés*, which they wanted to surround with suitably picturesque gardens. At the same time, in response to an increasing sensitivity to the world of nature, architects and garden designers such as Humphry Repton set about softening the boundaries between dwelling and garden with delightful contrivances such as conservatories, French windows, terraces and verandahs, with vases of flowers and plant containers in profusion both inside and out.

By the beginning of the nineteenth century both formal or informal flower gardens were popular. There had been a continuous, if eclipsed, tradition of flower gardens, but the vogue for informality owed much to William Mason's celebrated flower garden at Nuneham Courtenay, created in the 1770s, and was exemplified by Repton's own small garden in Essex, created in 1816. The inspiration for my design, however, comes mainly from Knowle Cottage in Devon, illustrated overleaf. My design has a central Repton flower basket flanked by two informal teardrop-shaped beds, which are based on plans in Maria Jackson's *The Florist's Manual* (1822). The beds are mounded up by about a foot, in the Repton manner, and are planted in descending order of height from the centre to the edges. 'Mingled' flower gardens such as this filled the beds with a variety of flowers, as opposed to the other custom then prevalent of dedicating each bed to a single species.

The containing shrubbery is based on a rare plan in J.C. Loudon's *Encyclopaedia of Gardening* (1822) which places spring flowers in the foreground; these can be replaced with later-flowering bulbs, perennials and even annuals. Being asymmetrical, this style can be adapted to any site, however awkward in shape, by simply moving or extending either the arrangement of trees and shrubs, or the beds.

The garden is roughly rectangular, 60 x 80 ft (18.3 x 24.4 m), and lies at the back or side of the house – though it could equally well be at the front – and falls gently in height away from the house. The verandah faces south, a principally southern aspect being essential for the success of any flower garden.

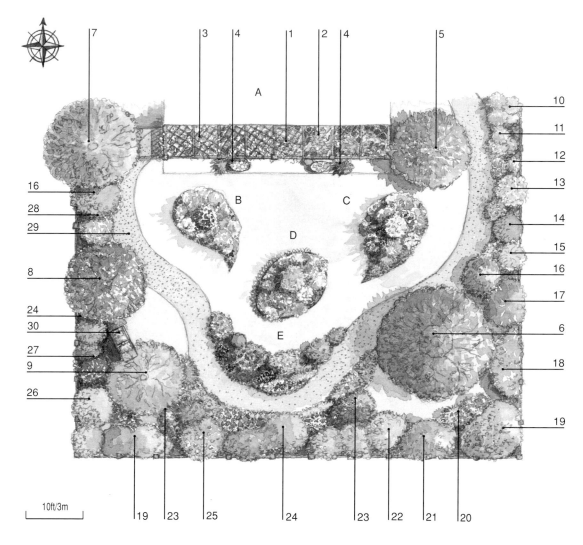

'Sibirica' (**18**), *Taxus baccata* (**19**), *Daphne mezereum* (**20**) *Pyracantha coccinea* (**21**), *Prunus laurocerasus* (**22**), *Ilex aquifolium* (**23**), *Viburnum tinus* (laurustinus) (**24**), *Viburnum opulus* (**25**), *Aucuba japonica* (**26**), *Rhamnus alaternus* (**27**), *Arbutus unedo* (**28**). The path (**29**) of binding gravel leads past two comfortable seats; a Gothick arbour (**30**) with a honeysuckle and a *Clematis viticella* climbing over it, and a tree seat round the walnut. Painted to match the trellis, both are of types which are commercially available today.

THE FLOWERBEDS

The three island flowerbeds (**B** - **D**), each at most 10-15 ft (3-4.5 m) across, need about 5 ft (1.5 m) between them, according to Maria Jackson in *The Florist's Manual*. They

BELOW A Gothick arbour such as this would be appropriate placed in any garden covering the period 1730 to 1830. It should be painted off-white, grey or sage green and enhanced with climbing flowering plants.

10ft/3m

THE VERANDAH

The simple trellis construction (**1**) has a vine (*Vitis vinifera*) (**2**) and a jasmine (*Jasminum officinale*) (**3**) for summer and autumn interest. Repton, who was responsible for the enormous popularity of trelliswork, recommends honeysuckles. A display of container flowers (**4**) adds to the charm of the effect; here they include *Agapanthus africanus* and fuchsias. A Judas tree (**5**), which has clusters of pink flowers, stands close to the house (**A**).

THE SHRUBBERY

The trees, chosen to give variety within a small space, include: a walnut (*Juglans regia*) (**6**); a crab apple (*Malus coronaria*) (**7**) which has white and pink flowers and green-yellow fruits; a mountain ash (*Sorbus aucuparia*) (**8**) which has white flowers and red fruits; and a weeping birch (*Betula pendula*) (**9**) which has silvery bark. Georgian and Regency shrubberies also had a foreground of seasonal flowers; bulbs, perennials and annuals and, in addition, potted and

bedding-out plants were used to fill the gaps. Make your choice (see page 149) bearing in mind the period predilection for hollyhocks, martagon lilies, columbines and foxgloves planted in groups and for roses planted in clumps. The planting on the plan includes *Rosmarinus officinalis* (**10**), *Phlomis fruticosa* (**11**), *Lavandula angustifolia* (**12**), *Syringa* × *persica* (**13**), *Buxus sempervirens* (**14**), *Genista tinctoria* (**15**), *Crataegus monogyna* (**16**), *Prunus lusitanica* (**17**) , *Cornus alba*

84

should be sited so they are visible from the windows of the house, and be banked up by about a foot (30 cm) at the centre. In the centre of beds **B** and **C** is a standard rose: the ancient Rosa Mundi, or the equally old 'Frankfurt rose' (*R. × francofurtana*) or the blush-white 'Félicité Perpétue', (1827). Around these are grouped other roses: the ancient 'Blush Damask', 'Tuscany' (1596), *R. × centifolia* 'Muscosa' (known in the late seventeenth century) and *R. centifolia* 'Cristata' (first recorded in about 1820). These are circled in descending order of height by pink Canterbury bells, white foxgloves, valerian, white *Lychnis chalcedonica alba*, white lupins and pink and white hollyhocks, with *Santolina chamaecyparissus, Lilium candidum, Astrantia major, Artemisia pontica, Campanula trachelium* 'Alba Flore Pleno', *Veronicastrum virginicum album* and white violas. The green-painted iron basket edging for bed **D** would need to be custom-made and is not essential, but the effect would be delightful. This contains the same flowers as beds **B** and **C** but with a *Rosa* 'Blush Noisette' at the centre. Bed **E** has been planted so that it can be appreciated from the path as well as from the house. It includes background evergreens such as *Juniper communis, J. virginiana* and *Euonymus americanus,* periwinkle for groundcover, a flowering shrub, *Daphne mezereum,* and other flowers such as sweet William, thrift, nigella, mignonette, campanula and antirrhinums which would have followed narcissus, fritillaries, snowdrops and muscari.

ABOVE Knowle Cottage at Sidmouth in Devon *c.*1834 was the main inspiration for my design. The lawns fall away from the cottage and are dotted with beds treated in the Repton manner. A conservatory houses tender plants, climbers clothe the walls and a path winds through the shrubbery.
RIGHT This complete garden from *The Florist's Manual* (1822) has serpentine beds cut into grass with trees and shrubbery around them.
BELOW The advent of the conservatory at the end of the eighteenth century signalled a huge interest in containers which were also used inside the house, on the porches and in the garden itself. This group by Humphry Repton includes clay pots, a wooden tub and more exotic wicker baskets.

Age of Opulence

1820~1890

E ngland's dominance in matters of garden design and style did not lessen as the nineteenth century progressed. The reason for this was primarily a social one: Britain was the first country in the world to experience an industrial revolution. This had a traumatic impact on all sections of society, and there was a general reaction of horror as factory chimneys and slum dwellings spread across the landscape. The small garden was born of that crisis. No other country in western Europe was to develop the townscapes that were to be- come typical of so much of Britain, consisting of terraces, semi-detached

A detail from Atkinson Grimshaw's painting *The Rector's Garden: Queen of the Lilies,* painted in 1877, showing the garden at Yew Court, Scalby, Yorkshire. This picture epitomizes what was called the old-fashioned garden, but which this was in fact very fashionable in the late Victorian period. It combines a nostalgic return to formality, as seen in the clipped box hedges, with a mixed planting – which was a reaction against the vogue for bedding out in blocks of colour..

and detached houses, each with its own patch of land for flowers and produce. Out of Britain, as a consequence of this, was to pour the earliest literature on the design and cultivation of small gardens, as horticulturists and writers combined to respond to a gigantic expansion in the number of gardens belonging above all to the middle classes.

The central figure in this development, whose shadow falls across the whole of the first half of the century, was John Claudius Loudon (1783-1843), who published some sixty million words on gardening and kindred topics during his lifetime. As had been the case in the garden revolution which had produced the landscape style, so in the revolution that followed it the new direction was to be signalled by a re-appraisal of attitudes to nature. It was Humphry Repton who towards the close of his career (he died in 1818) had declared 'Gardens are works of art rather than of nature'. This belief found expression in his work in a revival of formality and the creation of separate types of garden, combined with an acute historicizing streak, thus laying the foundations for the High Victorian style. Loudon, taking up the torch from Repton with a missionary zeal, translated these attitudes into forms which could find fulfilment in the new urban small gardens.

The period we are dealing with here stretches from about 1820 to 1890, by which time this style was already on the wane, yielding under pressure from William Robinson and his new naturalistic school. But from 1820 to 1860 it was on an upward curve, and the geometric formal garden proliferated. There was nothing new about the style, however, which instead consisted of a succession of pastiches in the styles of different countries and periods, reinterpreted in terms of contemporary planting. As in the decorative arts, the Victorians rampaged their way through the past, happily adopting the elements that appealed most from French baroque and rococo parterres, Elizabethan and Jacobean knot gardens and Italianate villa terraces and statuary alike. Though they inevitably differed in style, these gardens were united by the common factor of their formality, while at the same time proving to be ideal vehicles for a development that the plant revolution had made available to almost everyone by the 1850s: bedding out.

Bedding out was made possible by the mass cultivation of newly discovered and brightly coloured though tender plants mainly from South and Central America. Thanks to the recent development of commercial greenhouses, these could be cultivated under glass in enormous numbers, ready to be bedded out in May. Their reign of glory in the flower garden would last for some four months, until they were all pulled up with the onset of autumn. Pelargoniums, verbenas, dahlias, calceolarias and a whole lost range of other plants with brilliantly colourful flowers or foliage were arranged in bold geometric patterns set into smooth green turf, while dazzling colour combinations and patterns within each bed emphasized the overall shape and contributed further to the startling effect, which we still recognize as quintessentially Victorian.

This is not to say that the gardenesque tradition of the previous century did not survive. Perennial beds and borders continued to be made throughout the nineteenth century, although they were not to come back into the limelight until the closing years of the century. More common, certainly until the middle of the century, was the 'mingled' flower garden, a continuation of the late eighteenth-century tradition in which shrubs and herbaceous plants were mixed together. These were often planted in an arrangement of beds which was completely formal in plan and when planted later in the bedding-out style, these same beds would look totally different. The slender thread by which the 'mingled' flower garden tradition continued through the nineteenth century is an important one, for it shows that William Robinson and Gertrude Jekyll did not invent the herbaceous border but rather rediscovered and reorchestrated it for our own century.

Another development which began with Repton but only reached its full expression as the century progressed was the multiplication of different types of garden, each designed to be experienced separately. Next to the flower garden was the rose garden, again largely the result of an explosion in numbers of new varieties – literally hundreds of them – and also of the advent of repeat-flowering varieties, which extended an otherwise limited season. At the same time, in response to the influx of alpines, the rockery established itself as a separate garden or as a discreet part of a larger one; the

The rose garden at Warwick Castle, Warwick, was designed by Robert Marnock (1800-89) in 1869 and re-created in the 1980s. An enclosure backed by trees and evergreen shrubs and sited away from the castle, it is a classic example of the type, with verdant turf and box edging to set off the roses, and pillars, arches and swags to lift them upwards.

LEFT The flower garden at Audley End House, Cambridgeshire, was originally laid out by William Sawrey Gilpin in 1832 as a deliberate return to formality to match the Jacobean house. This re-creation of 1990 is the result of detailed archaeological and archival research, including original plant lists. In its planting the garden, which was in its heyday until about 1860, continued the eighteenth-century tradition of mingling together roses, perennials and annuals.

RIGHT The border at Arley Hall, Cheshire, one of a pair marked on a plan of 1840, demonstrates the development of the Victorian herbaceous border from the mixed borders of the Repton period. The continuing tradition was given new impetus by being 'rediscovered' by William Robinson and Gertrude Jekyll. At Arley the borders have handsome buttresses of yew.

'American' garden appeared, devoted solely to the shrubs, particularly the rhododendrons, of North America; and a craze for ferns reached its height in the 1850s.

The significance of the new phenomenon of gardening magazines can hardly be over estimated in terms of its impact on the development of the small garden. Loudon was again the pioneer, leading the way with his *Gardener's Magazine* (1826-44), which was followed by a huge growth in cheap, illustrated monthly periodicals with a mass circulation. It was a pattern that was to be repeated in Europe, and from 1859 Andrew Jackson Downing (1815-52), inspired by Loudon, edited the Gardeners Monthly in the United States. Books on the design and management of small gardens became best-sellers, and one of the earliest and most influential of this new breed of gardening writers was Shirley Hibberd (1825-90), who inherited all Loudon's enthusiasm for educating the middle classes in matters horticultural.

It was only in the nineteenth century that gardening in the United States really came of age, producing its first major figure in Andrew Jackson Downing, whose main achievement was nevertheless the naturalizing in North America of Loudon's work. Downing defined three styles: the old-fashioned or 'geometric', appropriate for public spaces and old houses; the 'beautiful' in which nature was tamed by the hand of art; and the 'picturesque', which reproduced the more violent, irregular and untamed aspects of nature. This meant the end of the old enclosed flower gardens and their replacement by irregular beds laid out along winding walks against a background of shrubs and trees: a belated version, in fact, of the gardenesque.

But the most important influence in the shaping of the American small garden was Frank J. Scott's *The Art of Beautifying Suburban Home Grounds of Small Extent* (1870). In his book, Scott formulated the principle which remains the chief difference between small gardens in Europe and America, according to which the whole of the front garden should be left unenclosed as continuous greensward for the enjoyment of the passer-by, with the house itself being

LEFT Mass bedding out of tender annuals for the summer months was a mid-Victorian innovation, to which municipal gardening has remained faithful ever since. Public parks in cities were a Victorian innovation and here at Lister Park, Bradford, Yorkshire, the planting continues to be in the manner of the last century, with masses of brilliantly coloured plants, including ageratum, grey *Senecio bicolor cineraria* and red and pink pelargoniums arranged in patterns.

RIGHT ABOVE An example of the same Victorian tradition today, in the spa town of Cheltenham, Gloucestershire, has an edging of chlorophytum enclosing scarlet salvias, with abutilons and standard fuchsias to add height to the composition.

RIGHT BELOW A re-creation in 1990 of carpet bedding in the Royal Horticultural Society's garden at Wisley, Sussex. Carpet bedding was an innovation of the 1870s, made possible by the introduction of new dwarf foliage plants from South America. The earth was mounded and a pattern laid out, generally in species of alternanthera, echeveria and sempervivum against a background of sedum. Among the most striking features of carpet bedding were its flatness, ideal for the display of pattern, and the marked subtlety of its colour range, particularly when compared with the hectic technicolour of bedding-out schemes.

framed by a foundation planting of evergreen shrubs. At the same time as it began assert its own horticultural identity, the United States, owing to the advent of the trans-atlantic steamboat, was effectively drawn closer to Europe. As a result a vast traffic in plants developed in the opposite direction.

Practicalities are easily forgotten, but their impact has always been enormous on the evolution of style. First in this period came the invention of the lawnmower, which was in mass production by the 1850s. As a result the lawn took on a new and central importance in the garden (a position from which it has never since been dislodged), becoming in its ideal form an immaculate piece of closely shorn and verdant turf. The advent of the hosepipe meant that watering on any scale was possible without great difficulty for the first time. New means of factory production meant that a huge range of hard structures for gardens became available in both cast iron and simulated stone and terracotta. Statues, urns, seats, tiling, fountains and edgings for beds could be purchased at modest prices to adorn what were deemed to be 'homes of taste'. There was a similar proliferation in ready-made rustic furniture, fencing and buildings in treated and painted wood. And wire, too, was produced in a range of pretty artefacts for both garden and conservatory, including aviaries, arbours, arches, plant supports and jardinières.

Greenhouses now became common. In England this was due above all to the development of plate glass and the abolition of the tax on glass, as a result of which both greenhouses and conservatories ceased to be the prerogative of the great house and began to grace the suburban villa. The greenhouse permitted the cultivation of Mediterranean fruits such as grapes, as well, of course, as the requisite number of bedding-out plants. The conservatory became a vehicle for exhibiting exotic plants brought back by plant hunters from the four corners of the earth. More welcome still was the fact that such heated enclosures ensured flowers for the house throughout the year.

This was also the golden age of the kitchen garden, which in the eighteenth century had been banished far from the house in order to avoid offending the inhabitants' eyes with the sight of such mundane practicalities, let alone of the servants at work. Now the kitchen garden became the subject of intense interest and study, and the fruits of the earth, including many exotic varieties, were cultivated with great skill for consumption virtually throughout the year. When discussing

LEFT The tradition of the *jardin-potager* mingling fruit, vegetables and flowers, goes back as far as the Renaissance. The potager at the Château de Saint-Jean-de-Beauregard, Isle-de-France, France, was originally laid out in the seventeenth century on lines identical to those of the *potager du roi* at Versailles. The area is quartered and then each section is quartered again; espaliered fruit trees form the 'walls' of the quarters and also act as a backdrop to a twentieth-century herbaceous border. The potager was re-created with modifications in 1985.

options for even the smallest town garden, Loudon always offered advice on how to plant it with fruit and vegetables for 'profit', and their inclusion in any garden of reasonable size was assumed to be a matter of course. The huge expansion in vegetable growing was greatly accelerated by the development of new improved varieties, which not only extended availability over longer periods of the year but also yielded produce of a higher quality.

The practice of gardening, especially on a small scale, enjoyed a position of high moral virtue in nineteenth-century society, involving as it did a great deal of honest and back-breaking labour to produce vegetables and flowers, the former being esteemed for their nutritional value and the latter for the sentimental significance with which the Victorians

invested them. It was a pursuit in which all sections of society could unite, from the lord in his castle to the humble cottager, a unifying factor of more than fanciful importance in an age which witnessed the extension of the franchise. Master and servant trod common ground in the garden, which was deemed to turn men's minds heavenwards, via Eden and Gethsemane, and certainly left them little time or energy for revolutionary politics. Women also found their place in the garden, for this was one of the few occupations worthy of even the most refined of fingers. But despite all this pious lip-service to morality, this is an era which remains conspicuous for its worship of Mammon, one of the prime expressions of which was an ostentatious, opulent and well-tended – not to say over-manicured – garden.

RIGHT The house and garden at Malleny
House, Balerno, Scotland, date back to
the sixteenth century, but the garden was
restored only at the close of the last
century, at the time of the revival of the
Scottish *jardin-potager* tradition. In the
potager gravel paths run between stone-
edged beds with a tumbling but ordered
mixture of deep mauve lavender, blue
borage, pastel-tinted sweet peas forming
a flowery wall, lettuces as edging and
cane wigwams for runner beans.

ABOVE A view of the herbaceous borders
at Malleny House, with a yew arch
leading to the vegetable garden beyond.
The border perennials tumble across the
path, leaving room for only one person to
squeeze past.

A NINETEENTH-CENTURY GARDEN OF THE DEEP SOUTH

Seen from a pergola on its east side, the flower garden measures 30 x 40 ft (9.1 x 12.2 m). Out of view, a second pergola on the north side leads to a kitchen garden and a service area.

This beguiling, enclosed garden with its contrasts of leafy shade and bright colours shows how the formal tradition of garden design never waned in the United States. Nowhere was this tradition stronger than in the south, where Spanish and French influences preceded the arrival of Anglo-Saxon-inspired ideas from the north; yet here, thanks to the exotic trees, shrubs and flowers which flourished in the hot, humid climate, it took on its own character. In New Orleans, Louisiana, where the sale of any property entailed the making of detailed plans not only of the house but also of the gardens, the Notarial Archives offer us a unique collection of designs for small gardens. This design is based on a plan dated 1844 (though both the building and the garden are likely to date from twenty years earlier) for a small garden attached to a modest Creole cottage. Into its tiny ground area, this garden manages to pack trees and flowers, shady pergolas and a kitchen garden.

It is a garden for warm climates, though with changes in planting its plan could be adapted for cooler ones. One of its most striking features is the wisteria-clad pergola which extends the line of the verandah over part of two of the flower beds. The verandah is the point of departure for the overall design of the garden, for it is from here that its beauties are to be savoured. There is therefore a strongly articulated vista from here across bright pink hibiscus, cooled by clipped evergreens, to a spiky yucca rising from a bed of multicoloured dahlias, a flower which was all the rage by the middle of the century, and a jasmine-covered arbour beyond. This is deliberately designed to be a garden of vivid colour, vibrant in the strong sunlight; its basic symmetry is offset by colourful, relaxed planting.

Running at right angles to the first pergola, which is hung with the lilac flowers of wisteria in early summer, is another one, also painted white, and entwined with a grape vine. Large enough to stroll in, with a comfortable seat at one end in which to linger, it also serves to divide the pleasure garden from the kitchen garden. It is a reminder that Louisiana was founded by the French in the eighteenth century, for this use of a *berceau* to divide the flower garden from the potager goes back three centuries to the garden described in *La Maison Rustique*.

This is not an expensive garden, once the initial landscaping has been done. The original paths may have been covered in crushed clam shells, but paving or brick are good alternatives. It is also reasonably low in maintenance: much of the planting is of trees, shrubs and perennials, and bulbs and annuals could be added to extend the flowering season.

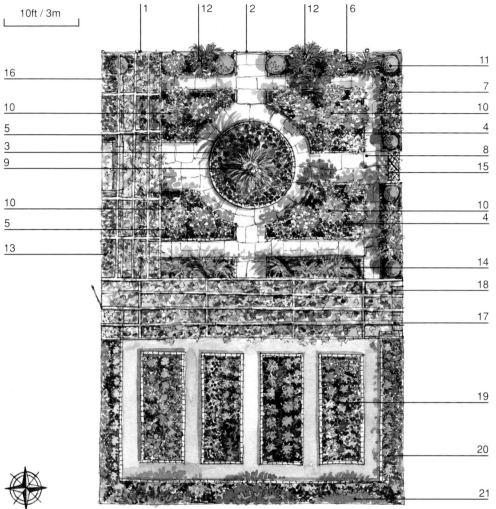

10ft / 3m

according to their aspect, but their design is held together by a series of clipped box balls (**11**). The north-facing entrance bed has two palm trees (*Livistona chinensis*) (**12**) rising above a planting of gardenias and day lilies. The west-facing border (**13**), in the shade of the verandah, is filled with ivy. The south-facing border (**14**) in front of the pergola has clumps of day lilies and agapanthus. The east-facing wall has an arbour (**15**) of sweet-smelling jasmine over a seat at its centre, and the beds (**7**) are filled with sunflowers (*Helianthus annuus*), which took over from a planting of bright poppies (*Eschscholzia californica*). The pergola (**16**) which abuts the verandah is covered with wisteria. The pergola, or *berceau*, to the north (**17**), which measures 40 x 8 ft (12.2 x 2.4 m) is covered with sweet grape vines (*Vitis rotundifolia*) and forms an open-air room with a seat at one end (**18**).

THE KITCHEN GARDEN
The kitchen garden, which measures about 40 x 20 ft (12.2 x 6.1 m), has four beds (**19**), each l5 x 5 ft (4.6 x 1.5 m) and a narrow 3 ft (90 cm) wide bed (**20**) beneath the fence. This narrow bed is edged with upturned and slanted bricks painted white, as in the flower garden. The centre beds are also edged with white-painted bricks, but this time laid straight. Narrow walks permit access for working. These four beds have space for herbs and a modest rotation of crops. Fig trees are planted along the long south-facing fence (**21**) and the flanking fences have espaliered peach and apple trees. In the beds beneath is space for more produce or a few flowers.

THE FLOWER GARDEN
The flower garden is partly hidden from the street by a fence with a *claire-voyée* (**1**) above it, and entered by a pretty Gothic gate (**2**). It is quartered, with a central circular bed (**3**) 12 ft (3.6 m) in diameter, surrounded by four spandrel beds, two (**4**) 8 x 13 ft (2.4 x 3.7 m) and two (**5**) 6 x 13 ft (1.8 x 3.7 m). Beneath the south (**6**) and west (**7**) garden walls are narrow beds 3 ft (90 cm) wide, edged with

slanting upended bricks painted white. The paths (**8**) are paved, though brick or pea gravel would be good alternatives. The centre bed has as its focal point a *Yucca gloriosa* (**9**), which is surrounded in spring by tulips (which will need pre-cooling in a refrigerator for 6-8 weeks before planting in places as warm as New Orleans) and in late summer by dahlias. An alternative and equally dramatic centrepiece would be an agave or century plant; and four

o'clocks (*Mirabilis jalapa*) would make a multicoloured perennial fringe. The spandrel beds (**4** and **5**) are dominated by four brilliant pink *Hibiscus syriacus* trained as standards. Most of the rest of the space is filled with hydrangeas and a sprinkling of zinnias and, in the shade, the fronds of *Nephrolepis exaltata*. Any remaining spaces should be filled in spring with bulbs and in summer with annuals. The beds around the sides are treated variously,

ABOVE Instead of a kitchen garden, the same space could be planted as a shady shrubbery walk. This one has gravel walks, while the beds are once more edged with slanted, upended, white-painted bricks. The focus of the centre bed is a mulberry tree (*Morus alba multicaulis*). (Between 1826 and 1841, the years of the silk boom, more mulberries were planted in this region than probably any other tree.) A flowering almond or a pomegranate would be an attractive alternative. On either side are roses: *Rosa foetida* and *R.ruqosa*. The spandrels are planted with two handsome wax myrtles (*Myrica cerifera*), two firs, and a mixed planting of evergreen and flowering shrubs including gardenia, oleander and viburnum for year-round interest, and there are spaces for foreground planting if desired.

ABOVE AND RIGHT This tiny New Orleans Creole cottage and its ground-plan, recorded in 1844, were the sources for my design, and reveal the formal structure of these gardens and the premium attached to pergolas for shade. The pretty railings include a door giving access to the street.

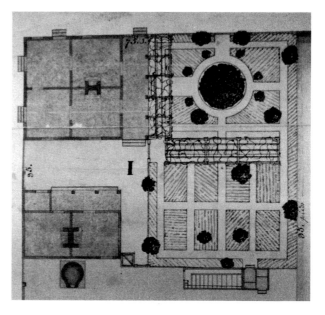

LEFT This detail from a ground-plan of another New Orleans property of 1847 inspired my alternative design. It shows an alternative way of laying out a formal flower garden, and includes a shrubbery walk – a descendant of the seventeenth century but with a touch of the English landscape style which had percolated even the French formal tradition of Louisiana by this time.

A MID-VICTORIAN ROSE GARDEN

The sight of a swagged and garlanded rose garden blooming *en masse* would be breathtaking; and for sheer garden spectacle, matchless. Little wonder that no garden of any size would have been considered complete in the mid-nineteenth century without a rose garden. Encouraged by the exciting expansion in varieties during the first half of the century, roses – hitherto part of the foreground of the shrubbery – became the subject of a separate garden. Today a rose garden can earn its place in, or as, a small garden because the flowering season of modern roses is so much longer, and because with good structure and good underplanting, it can be interesting throughout the year.

The most famous of the early rose gardens was created between 1804 and 1809 by the Empress Josephine at Malmaison. In England the rise in popularity of the rose garden was to go hand in hand with a return to formality, heralded by Humphry Repton's design dated 1813 for a circular rosarium at Ashridge in Hertfordshire, where petal-shaped beds radiated from a central fountain and were enclosed by rose arches. In 1812, J.C. Loudon printed two designs for rose gardens, one oval and the other octagonal, and both echoing Repton's formality. The key work for the period, however, is William Paul's *The Rose Garden* (1848) which endorses the view that the ideal framework for roses was formality:'parallelograms, square, circles, ovals and other regular figures...display the Roses to the greatest Advantage'. To this he added a strong preference for beds cut into grass 'which sets off the plants, when in flower, to much greater advantage than gravel'.

My design, however, is based on one in Edward Kemp's influential *How to Lay Out a Garden* (1850), where the garden is set among an evergreen planting of conifers, but is surrounded more immediately by a collection of hollies, which contribute contrasting foliage and bright berries to the composition. A successful Victorian rose garden depends largely on a strong and symmetrical ground-plan, together with the use of enough structural vertical features to coax the roses upwards. The heaviest financial outlay would be the iron pillars, chains and arches, which should ideally be custom-built and set in concrete. Though several versions are now available in synthetic materials, which are considerably cheaper, they are far less attractive. Larch poles and rope would make reasonable rustic alternatives, though less durable. In terms of maintenance, the garden will require pruning, tying in, feeding, weeding and path clearing.

A rose garden must be sited in a sunny and sheltered spot. In the Victorian period, this was traditionally within an informal shrubbery, mainly of evergreens (the enclosure by a yew hedge was an innovation associated with Gertrude Jekyll and her era). This one is 40 ft (12.2 m) in diameter, but would benefit from being larger in order to increase the size of the central grass area and the four oval beds.

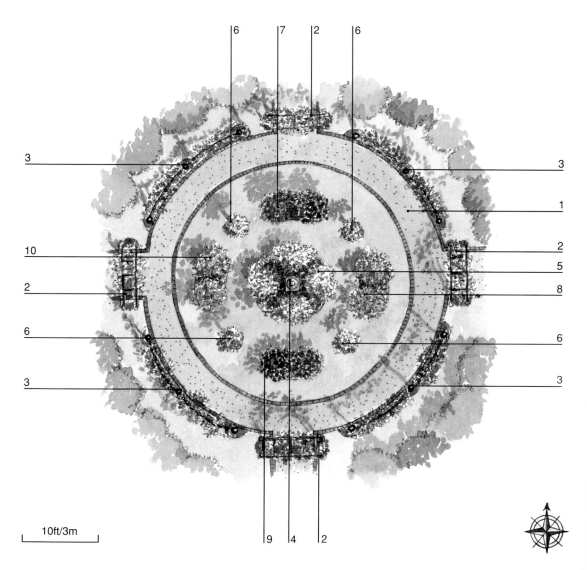

10ft/3m

THE ROSES

The layout contains 36 roses in white, pink and red/maroon (yellows began to appear only after the middle of the century), all grouped according to type as prescribed by Loudon. You will need to adapt your scheme according to the availability of roses in your area, but keeping to a restricted colour palette. In catalogues of old roses you will sometimes find the date of the introduction of a new rose varies by a few years. Because

so many authentic period roses have short-lived flowering times, you could use modern repeat-flowering roses of the type now bred by David Austin, which look like the old varieties and retain the same delicacy of colour.

THE CIRCULAR WALK

The garden is encompassed by a circular gravel walk (**1**), 5 ft (1.5 m) wide and edged with brick. There are four entrances, each under an arch (**2**) about 6 ft (1.8 m) wide and 8 ft (2.4 m)

high clothed with the double white Noisette rose 'Aimée Vibert' (1828). One or more of these arches could be made into an arbour with a seat. The pillars and garlands (**3**) form a continuous frieze of the deep pink Bourbon rose, 'Zéphirine Drouhin' (1868), which holds the composition together.

THE CENTRAL BED

The central bed is 10 ft (3 m) in diameter with an urn (**4**) about 6 ft (1.8 m) high positioned so that it can be seen from a

distance through the entrance arches. Happily there are several exact reproductions from the period available in reconstituted stone. The urn could be replaced with a group of standard roses – as Loudon advocated – but at the cost of year-round sculptural interest. The urn is surrounded by four white Alba roses (**5**): 'Alba Maxima' the Jacobite rose, (an ancient variety), 'Mme Legras de Saint Germain' (before 1848), 'Mme Plantier' (1835) and 'Alba Semiplena' (ancient).

THE CIRCULAR BEDS

Four white standard weeping 'Félicité Perpétue' (1827) (**6**), are planted in separate beds on their own as Kemp recommended. Here the beds are 3 ft (90 cm) in diameter, and the roses underplanted with lavender (or use violas).

THE OVAL BEDS

Each measures about 8 x 4 ft (2.4 x 1.2 m), and contains roses of one type in a restricted colour range. If you are able to enlarge the scheme, add more roses of the same type and colour to each bed. One of the beds (**7**) contains moss roses in shades of crimson, maroon and purple: 'Capitaine John Ingram' (1854) and 'Nuits de Young' (1845). Next to it is a bed (**8**) of pink Damask roses 'Celsiana' (before 1750) and 'La Ville de Bruxelles' (1849), or you could substitute 'Marie Louise' (Malmaison, 1813) or 'Quatre Saisons' (ancient). Opposite the dark moss roses is a bed (**9**) of Gallicas also in crimson, maroon and purple: 'Tuscany Superb' (before 1845) and 'D'Aguesseau' (1823), or you could substitute 'Cardinal de Richelieu' (Lafayette 1840), or 'Président de Sèze' (c.1836). The fourth bed (**10**) again echoes

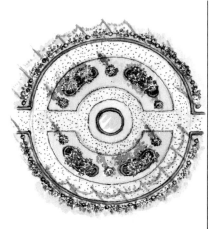

ABOVE The alternative design, with only two entrances, has a central box-edged bed filled with standard roses and surrounded by four more long beds, also edged with box and dedicated to a single type, interspersed with pillar roses. In place of rose garlands the garden is contained by arches, also now available commercially in synthetic materials.

the pink opposite, but in Provence roses: *Rosa × centifolia* 'Cristata' (Chapeau de Napoléon) (1827) and *R. × centifolia* (ancient). If the rose garden is your only garden, you will almost certainly want to extend interest back to spring and forward to late summer; and to do so would be perfectly in period. The following advice is quoted by William Paul from the Leeds-based firm of landscape gardeners, Major & Son: '...the beds might be planted with patches of early flowering bulbs, to precede the general bloom of Roses; which bulbs, after flowering, might be lifted, and their places supplied by all the different kinds of Annuals, to succeed the general Rose bloom. So that there would first be a show of early bulbs and flowers; then a grand display of Roses; and lastly, the show of Annuals'.

ABOVE A watercolour by Thomas Hunn of the rose garden at Clandon, Surrey, in the late Victorian period. A central pool mirrors the flowers on the surrounding rose arches. The flanking beds contain bush and standard roses as well as climbers trained up pillars. The design is typically geometric and symmetrical, making use of curves and supports to carry the flowers upwards.
BELOW Four forms of rose support available from the Pyghtle Works c.1910. These would have been a combination of iron and wood painted green. Similar styles are now beginning to become available again.

A VICTORIAN BACK GARDEN

This garden, kept in artful order, will reward you with a picture of domestic prettiness worthy of a Victorian valentine. With its curious mixture of order and disorder, light and dark, the puritanical and the sensuous, it reflects the preoccupation of an age in which stern moral values were combined with a rather maudlin sentimentality. The re-creation of a garden like this presents few problems, for in a sense the ingredients of the style have never quite left us. The basic structure of many original gardens can still be detected, as if they are waiting to be brought back to life. The same plants or their modern counterparts are still available today, as are many of the artefacts, both originals and reproductions.

Tiny gardens, often rectangular in shape, were a common feature of the urban building boom of the era. The first occupants of these houses made up a huge new market, hungry for information on gardening and catered for by a plethora of new periodicals on horticultural matters. Among the most influential and prolific of all writers on small urban gardens was Shirley Hibberd (1825-90), author of the universely popular *Rustic Adornments for Homes of Taste*, which was first published in 1856 and went through many editions.

My design is inspired by Hibberd's description of his notion of an ideal layout for 'even the smallest of suburban or town gardens, measuring say from sixty to ninety feet in length, from twenty to thirty in breadth'. The style, while purporting to be a blend of art and nature, is fundamentally one of pure artifice. Dubbed by Loudon the 'gardenesque', by the 1850s and 60s this style was reaching the peak of its popularity. But let Hibberd speak for himself: 'It is laid out with a central grass-plot, in which are one central oval, and two small circular beds. Around the walls runs a narrow border, separated from the grass plot by a continuous path. The walls must be covered with ivy, clematis, jasmine, and other climbers ... Let the border under the rear wall be raised into a bank... the rock-work is so arranged that there are plenty of interstices for the insertion of plants in front. Now in one corner place a syringa or a holly, and in the other a few rhododendrons. A white poplar, birch, or tree of any kind, will be an improvement if planted towards one side'.

The wall behind should be planted with jasmine, ivy or Virginia creeper, indeed anything 'dark'. The bank itself should be scattered with spring flowers, to be followed in summer by 'bright verbenas, heliotropes, hawkweeds, yellow and white alyssum, and in one corner ivy, which should be trailed over

Strong colour and pattern were the two essential features of the planting of any Victorian flower garden: here white standard roses, 'Félicité Perpétue' arise from a carpet of red pelargoniums edged with lobelia and alyssum.

the stone into a rich knoll, so as to contrast with the flowers beside it'. This is a recipe for a south-facing wall. Ours is north-facing, however, or as Hibberd would describe it, 'a dark bowery spot where light is wanted'. For such situations he recommends the use of white stones, to which I have added a collection of that typically Victorian plant, the fern, and other shade-loving plants.

In the main lawn I have incorporated two asymmetrical flowerbeds which echo the curves of the surrounding path. Mid-Victorian flowerbeds either continued the gardenesque tradition of loose, informal shapes within serpentine walks, or symmetrical, geometric shapes if set within a rectanglar or square lawn. The beds are treated in the quintessentially Victorian manner: planted with brightly coloured annuals massed in patterns, a feature known as bedding out. You can, of course, dispense with the beds altogether if you require an uninterrupted lawn.

I have also included an arbour with a rustic seat, ceramic rope-edged tiles to retain the beds, terracotta urns, an entrance arch, and a sentimental statue which presides calmly over the scene. All these ingredients are available in reproduction and can, of course, be rearranged within the same scheme.

This rockwork, which faces north, is at the end of a typically rectangular urban back garden which measures 60 x 25 ft (18.3 x 7.6m).

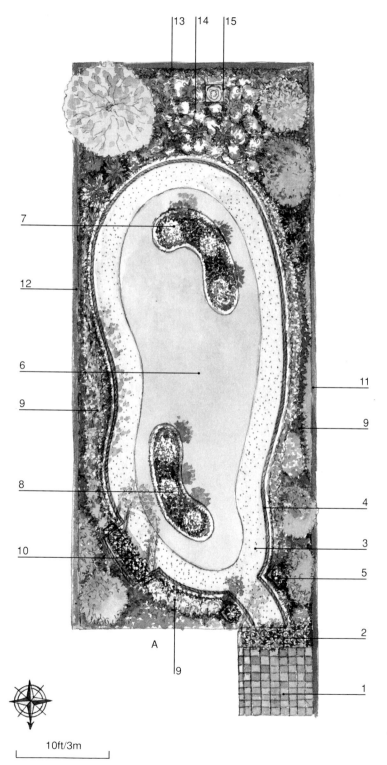

10ft/3m

The approach from a small terrace (**1**) is through a wire arch (**2**) over which clambers a *Clematis × jackmanii,* which bears violet-blue flowers throughout the summer months. This leads on to a narrow gravel path (**3**), 3 ft (90 cm) wide, bordered with ceramic rope-edged tiles (**4**). Although these are available in reproduction, they are not essential and up-ended or diagonally-placed old bricks would be equally appropriate. Terracotta urns (**5**) filled with trailing white pelargoniums flank the entrance to the garden. The path surrounds a central lawn (**6**) in which two curving beds (**7** and **8**) are bedded out in red, white and blue (see previous page). For those who need the maximum area of grass, a typical Victorian solution would be to make the lawn rectangular with straight paths and narrow peripheral borders and, instead of the asymmetrical island beds, to cut narrow ribbon beds – broken by small circular beds for standard or pillar roses at the corners – just inside the parameters of the lawn. The borders (**9**) are also lined with white alyssum, but backed by a mixture of plants including yellow antirrhinums, white Madonna lilies (*Lilium candidum*), pale yellow hollyhocks and an *Elaeagnus angustifolia,* which also bears creamy flowers in early summer. Other typical Victorian flowers which could be incorporated include *Dicentra spectabilis,* Japanese anemones, Solomon's seal (which would be happy among the ferns), geum, peonies, *Phlox paniculata* 'Alba' and *Iris germanica.* Near the house (**A**) is a rustic seat (**10**) beneath a

wire arbour (or one of rustic larch poles if you prefer), with a creamy white rose, *R.* 'Climbing Sombreuil', and a honeysuckle over it. In spring the lilac (*Syringa × persica*) behind will contribute its heady scent. Victorian-style arbours and arches are now available in synthetic materials, try to check the authenticity of their design.

THE WALLS

Trellis, stained with preservative, brings the overall height of the walls to about 7 ft 6 in (2.3 m) and the abundant use of climbers creates a degree of privacy. The east wall (**11**) has a pyracantha and a variegated ivy; the west wall (**12**) a Virginia creeper (*Parthenocissus quinquefolia*); and the south wall (**13**) dark green ivies and a jasmine (*Jasminum officinale*), arranged so as to frame the statue.

THE ROCKERY

The rockwork (**14**) rises 3 ft 6 in (1.1 m) to 4 ft (1.2 m) against the wall and, as it faces north, is of light-coloured stones. A sentimental statue (**15**) is placed in the centre as a focal point, flanked in one corner by a silver birch tree (*Betula papyrifera*) and in the opposite one by a golden-edged holly (*Ilex aquifolium*) and a yellow azalea (*Rhododendrun luteum*). The rockwork is smothered with trailing ivies, sempervivums, hostas and ferns. For spring interest, scatter-plant bulbs such as crocus, hyacinths, narcissi and snowdrops, with lily of the valley and martagon lilies for later in the year. For those who do not wish to make a rockery, a dense shrubbery – mainly of evergreens – would be more ordinary, but equally period, alternative.

ABOVE A rare early colour print showing the rockery in the Horticultural Society's gardens in the 1850s. The planting is a mixture of dwarf conifers, a yucca, annuals such as foxgloves, Solomon's seal and small alpine plants. BELOW A view down a Victorian back garden at its apogee in 1875. Privacy from prying neighbours is assured by heavy plantings of evergreens on either side which also act as a backdrop to the massive patterned bedding out scheme predominantly in red, white and grey. The garden path straddled by an iron pergola is only at one side to ensure the largest possible area of immaculately kept lawn. At the end of the garden are the greenhouses.

ABOVE AND BELOW Garden seats and tables in wood and iron, and a decorative iron arch, all in commercial manufacture during the late Victorian era, recorded in Harrods department store catalogue, 1895. Similar styles are available again today.

A VICTORIAN FLOWER GARDEN

The spectacular, often highly intricate floral mosaics that were created in the mid-nineteenth century epitomize the Victorian feeling for colour and concern for decorative detail; and they aptly complement the strong architectural features of the period. Perhaps best suited nowadays to front gardens – which are often smaller yet more noticed – the stunning effect of brilliantly coloured flowers and leaves arranged in patterns would be fun to create, eye-catching and unquestionably period.

It was in the Victorian era that the flower garden reached its heyday, a development which set gardens of the period firmly apart from their predecessors. The new interest in flowers symbolized a dramatic change of emphasis in garden-making, away from the eighteenth-century concern with form and line and towards a preoccupation with colour. Of the many phases that the flower garden went through, the one which was uniquely Victorian, was bedding out. The advent of the greenhouse enabled commercial nurseries to grow tender annuals in their thousands ready to be planted out for the summer months. With their dazzling colours, new flowers such as calceolarias, salvias and lobelias opened up exciting possibilities for making patterns in the garden. Strong colour, now out of fashion, was then both novel and exhilarating. This robustness of taste was not of course confined to the garden; it is obvious in interior decoration and can perhaps be seen at its most vibrant in the paintings of the Pre-Raphaelites, which are well worth the attention of anyone who is thinking of planting a Victorian flower garden.

The garden in late summer bedded out with an edging of grey *Senecio bicolor cineraria* and filled with red *Begonia semperflorens* and purple *Verbena rigida*, with a red *Phormium tenax* as a vertical centrepiece.

The fashion for massing plants with brightly coloured flowers and leaves of every shade of green, yellow, red and purple, developed in the gardens of the great country houses during the 1830s. It was encouraged by the introduction over the previous twenty years or so of many half-hardy and tender annuals, most of which came from the Americas. While they feuded fiercely over details, garden writers of the period were categorical about the ideal plan for a flower garden. It should have a southerly aspect and be set in smooth verdant turf – in itself another novelty, this time made possible by the advent of the lawnmower. The patterns were invariably strictly geometric, which makes it quite easy to invent designs remembering only to observe enough space to allow a lawnmower to be used between the beds. Inspiration for designs and planting can be found in many gardening books of the period, one of the most influential of which, Shirley Hibberd's *The Amateur's Flower Garden* (1871), now exists in reprint. The designs here are simplifications of ones in *Plans for Flower Gardens, Beds, Borders, Rosaries, and Aquariums* (c.1874), published by the *Journal of Horticulture*.

For the Victorians there was only one drawback to such a flower garden: it would have been empty from October until May. To compensate for this, winter bedding out was also used. Deciduous and evergreen shrubs, chosen for their winter and early spring interest in terms of leaf colour, berries and flowers, would be put in the beds in October, together with bulbs for the spring, and then lifted and transferred to another area of the garden for the summer months, when more colourful and exotic summer bedding plants took centre stage. As so few people have room to store alternative seasonal planting, I have suggested an amalgamation of these two approaches by introducing evergreen vertical accents and edging as permanent features and changing the floral interest from spring bulbs, through annuals (and some herbaceous perennials) to autumn pansies. The important thing to remember is to keep the patterns obvious and, ideally, to let no earth be visible. Present taste in colour is much in favour of muted softness but to be truly Victorian your colour should be strong, though not necessarily unrestrained. Two rules are useful for exerting a measure of control: the first is to pay due attention to the cooling properties of the greens in the leaves of bedding and border plants, and the second is to use yellow only in the outer beds and never at the centre. This will also make the flower garden look larger than it is.

The beds are cut into a smooth lawn, and the scheme is 15 ft (4.5 m) square.
If you have room you could increase the proportions to 25 ft (7.6 m) square,
or double or even quadruple the design. Any flower garden calls for a
southerly aspect; this one faces south-east.

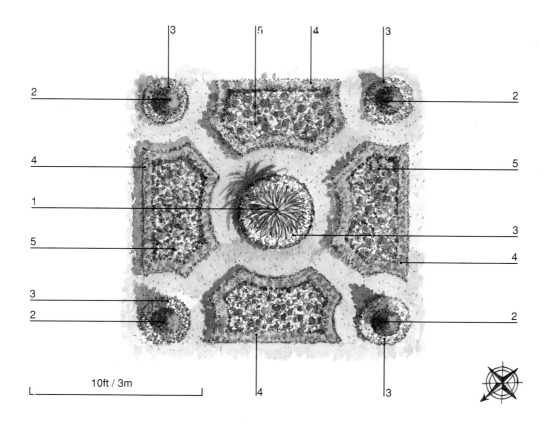

ABOVE For those who would like the challenge of being truly authentic, this alternative, more complex design relies for its jewel-like effect on being bedded out with annuals for the summer months. The four spandrel beds are edged with dwarf white geraniums, and two are filled with scarlet pelargoniums and two with yellow calceolarias. The outer hexagonal beds are edged with grey *Cerastium tomentosum* and filled with blue lobelia. The centre bed is again edged with dwarf white geraniums which enclose dwarf purple fuschias, and a tall standard fuschia stands at the centre. You can easily make your own scheme – and indeed change it from year to year in terms of both colour and plants – keeping to certain guide lines: the border plants should be low; those within the beds should be of equal height; no earth should be visible; introduce one or more vertical accents; bank up the beds, especially at the centre; aim for colour balance, but not in mirror image terms; and never place yellow at the centre.

THE BEDS

The flower list on page 151 contains a section on plants suitable for both the centres and the borders of such beds. Beds continued to be banked up in the middle, with the central bed often more steeply banked than the others. In planting, graduations of height are important: the edging plants must be low and those at the centre taller. I have used a *Phormium tenax* (**1**), which was one of the more exotic introductions to the Victorian garden from New Zealand, in the middle to provide a powerful focal point. A standard fuchsia would be an alternative for the summer but would need

replacing in the winter. Four dwarf conifers in the corner beds (**2**) hold the design and give important vertical accents to the composition. The four circular corner beds and the central bed are edged in *Bellis perennis* (**3**) which, if kept well clipped, will provide a neat band of evergreen leaves for the rest of the year. To be more in period, however, this should be replaced with an annual edging plant such as *Senecio bicolor cineraria* in the summer. The other four beds are edged in evergreen *Euonymus japonicus* 'Microphyllus' (**4**) which, again, could be replaced with summer annuals such as alyssum for more floriferous interest. These

beds are block-planted for a late spring display of wallflowers and pink tulips (**5**). A different scheme might include bright coloured tulips and forget-me nots. Late in the summer you could replace these with a mixture of red begonias and purple *Verbena rigida* to achieve the 'shot silk' effect that was so admired at the time. The Victorians aimed for symmetry and balance in their planting. The effect should be one of a sumptuous mosaic of brilliant colour typical of the High Victorian period. To achieve this I would counsel buying or growing more plants than you need and keeping a few by to cope with disasters.

RIGHT A flower garden with winter bedding at Heckfield Place, 1884. During the winter the summer bedding display was replaced by a winter one in which evergreen shrubs in pots were plunged into the beds. Hollies, skimmia, mahonia, gaultheria and cotoneaster were favourite plants. Here the system is seen at its apogee and was described by the *Gardener's Chronicle* of 1884 as having 'neat designs worked out...in golden Hollies, Aucubas, small Conifers, Euonymus, Heaths, ... carpets of Sedums and Herniaria'.

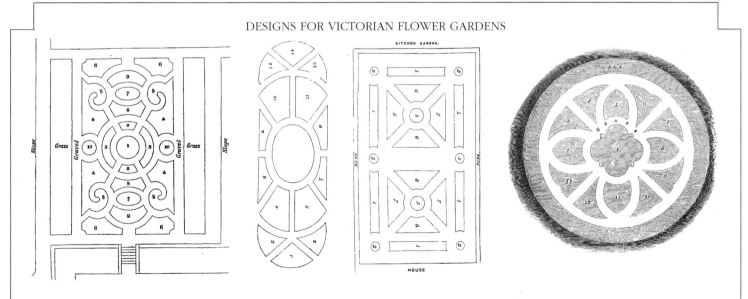

DESIGNS FOR VICTORIAN FLOWER GARDENS

On the left is a design for a sunken garden from *The Amateur's Flower Garden* (1871) by Shirley Hibberd; the three designs on the right are from *Plans for Flower Gardens, Beds and Borders* by contributors to the *Journal of Horticulture* (c.1874). All the beds are either cut into grass or set against gravel, and would have been bedded out in symmetrical blocks of colour with the addition of edging plants and vertical accents such as pillar roses or fuchsias, and sometimes a central bed of roses. The plants most often advocated were verbenas, lobelia, petunias, pelargoniums, calceolarias, heliotrope, plants with exotic coloured leaves such as amaranthus and coleus, and edgings of alyssum, lobelia, *Cerastium tomentosum* and

A TRADITIONAL SCOTTISH POTAGER

At its height, the country house kitchen garden, with its espaliered or cordoned fruit trees, its rows of vegetables, its greenhouses, compost heaps and wide herbaceous borders, was a fine garden type in its own right. While it belongs to the history of large gardens, it is also one of the most appealing ways of treating a small site because it combines, instead of separates, the decorative and productive aspects of gardening. Borders of flowers or avenues of trained fruit trees, used to conceal the vegetables, also make a delightful contrast to the vegetables.

This tradition of the combination of fruit, flowers and vegetables goes back at least as far as the Renaissance, and was carried on for centuries in the less grand gardens of northern Europe which remained untouched by the whims of fashion. The concept of a garden laid out neatly along the lines of a vegetable garden, but including fruit and flowers, is still particularly strong in France where it is known as a *jardin de curé*.

Towards the end of the nineteenth century the designer Robert Lorrimer (1864-1929) acquired the castle of Kellie in Scotland where he found 'flowers, fruit and vegetables... all mixed up together'; seizing on the idea, he became responsible for the revival of the traditional mixed kitchen garden in this decorative form. These gardens were generally walled and square or rectangular, with the longest axis running east–west in order to provide a long south-facing wall for the ripening of fruit. There is an alternative, however: at Birkhall in Aberdeenshire, a residence of Queen Elizabeth the Queen Mother, there is a mixed kitchen garden (not designed by Lorimer) which makes use of hedges instead of walls, and is also exceptional in being semicircular, or rather bell-shaped. The design given here is inspired by Birkhall but on a greatly reduced scale. It is intended for the dedicated gardener, for the raising of fruit and vegetables is labour-intensive, though richly rewarding. Here the flower borders lie at the heart of the garden and the path that bisects it leads to a topiary centre-piece and on to a summerhouse. This symmetry is broken in the vegetable beds by a healthy irregularity in the siting of narrow paths (governed by convenience) and of the fruit frame and greenhouse. By its very nature this is principally a summer and autumn garden, but bulbs could be planted in the grass areas and in the borders to give spring interest. The topiary, of course, will bring year-round pleasure. The siting of the garden assumes the presence of large trees or buildings in the vicinity to act as a windbreaks.

This is not an expensive garden to make, as it consists only of brick, gravel, grass, hedging and topiary evergreens, with an optional summerhouse and greenhouse. Patience for up to ten years will be necessary for the topiary to reach maturity, although as there are only five pieces it might be possible to buy large specimens. The surrounding tapestry hedge, however, would certainly need five to eight years before it approached perfection. A rabbit fence of close meshed wire, sunk 2 ft (60 cm) below the surface of the earth and rising 3 ft (90 cm) above it, is essential if the fruits of your labours are not to be decimated.

Traditionally sited away from the house, and enclosed to provide protection from the weather and wild animals, a mixed vegetable and flower garden like this is easily decorative enough to place beside the house. The hedge here has a diameter of about 160 ft (48.8 m); and its longest extent is on an east-west axis, so that there is ample space appropriate for growing fruit on a southerly aspect.

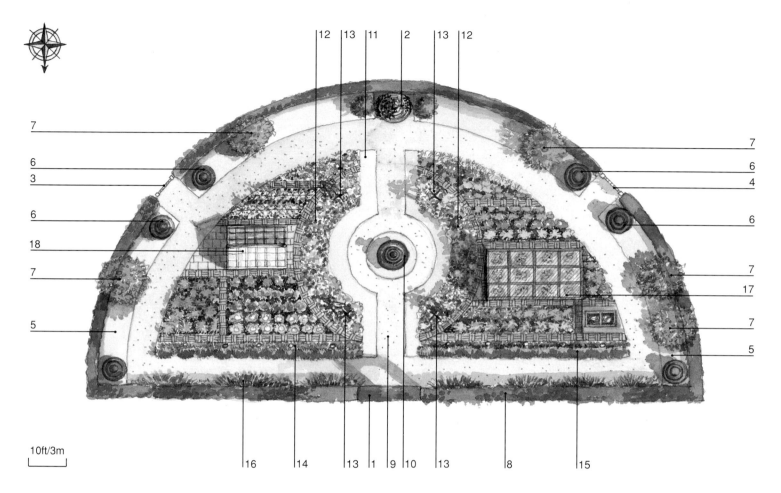

10ft/3m

The main entrance (**1**) to the garden is in the south-facing hedge, although ideally it should be in the opposite one, to allow the maximum room for sun-loving fruit trees; but it would be a simple matter to exchange positions with the summerhouse (**2**). The other entrances (**3** and **4**) are optional, but the belt of grass (**5**) definitely calls for some enlivening: here I have suggested using topiary sentinels (**6**), as well as some dwarf-rooted fruit trees (**7**), including, perhaps, a quince or medlar. The summerhouse (**2**), based on a contemporary design, has evergreen shrubs on either side and climbers scrambling over its roof. The surrounding tapestry hedge (**8**) is a mixture of holly, yew, beech and common quickthorn. Beech, hornbeam and yew would make a good alternative. The top of the hedge is straight, but you may wish to enliven it by introducing piers either side of the gates, or cutting it into swags or crenellations; but keep the shapes bold and simple. If you can afford to build a wall, do so along the south-facing side and use it to support espaliered fruit trees. Although I have suggested planting grass (**5**) beneath the semicircular hedge, a vast flower border would not only look ravishing but would be a more correct option if you have the energy and the means. The inner half-circle is surrounded and bisected by a broad gravel path (**9**) 8 ft (2.4 m) wide. A topiary yew (**10**) provides a focal point. An alternative would be a Portugal laurel (*Prunus lusitanica*) trained as an umbrella, or perhaps a stone wellhead. The band of grass (**11**) each side of the central path sets off herbaceous borders (**12**) which are 8 ft (2.4 m) wide and would be even better if they were wider still. I have included wigwams for clematis (**13**) to give added height to the borders; but an alternative would be to back them with rose garlands or arches, or a screen of espaliered fruit trees. The planting will depend on your colour choice, but the height should be graded up from the front. As you will also see the border from the periphery path, you should consider the view from there too. If this is your only space for flowers, a mixed border of evergreen shrubs, perennials, bulbs and annuals would give you year-round interest. Along the south walk are horizontally-trained pear and apple trees (**14**), which would require a strong frame to support them initially. Such a frame could be constructed of trellis battened to larch poles or, simpler still, it could be a series of posts with horizontal wires run at intervals onto which to tie the branches. I have suggested underplanting the front trees with a border of lavender (**15**) to make a scented walk; if space allowed, you could plant another border on the opposite side of the walk. Here there is just room for self-seeding annuals such as valerian and nepeta (**16**). The main vegetable areas are divided by narrow brick paths to provide access to the beds, and to the soft fruit cage (**17**) and greenhouse (**18**). The design of fruit cages has not changed much in the intervening years, but a period design for the greenhouse would be essential. The allocation of space to vegetables, herbs and other produce will vary according to individual preference, bearing in mind the needs of the plants. Here these are artichokes, cauliflowers, spinach, potatoes, leeks, salad greens and runner beans on canes.

LEFT Herbaceous border in a watercolour by Helen Allingham (1848-1926). This is a wide border which might be used to line the central path of a mixed kitchen garden, with the flowers graduated according to height and including an abundance of late summer and autumn purples and yellows: heleniums, helianthus, rudbeckia and Michaelmas daisies.

BELOW LEFT Yew hedges, topiary and a spring border at Mathern, *c.*1912: an example of the type of sculptured yew and profusion of flowers that became so popular in the early twentieth century. To copy this you might consider buying topiary yew sentinels 4 or 5 ft (1.2-1.5 m) high but lower hedging plants to obtain an immediate effect. The planting here is a spring one of tulips and forget-me-nots, and would have been followed by a range of herbaceous plants and annuals.

BELOW Two wooden summerhouses. The octagonal one comes from J.P. White's Pyghtle Works catalogue of *c.*1910; the thatched circular example comes from *Garden Planning* (1910) by W.S. Rogers.

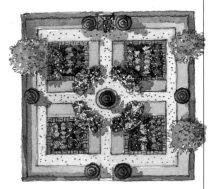

ABOVE A similar garden could be a based on a square or rectangle quartered by two crossing paths — but if you don't have four entrances, include a focal point at the end of at least one path

Age of Nostalgia

1890~1940

*T*he period running from the last decade of the nineteenth century to the end of the 1930s was dominated by a single event, the First World War, which had a profound effect on every aspect of life in Europe, including gardening. Nothing was ever to be the same again. The war brought disruption, but more significantly it signalled the end of the essentially hierarchical class system that had conditioned the nature of garden-making in Europe since the Renaissance. Royal and aristocratic gardening vanished or atrophied, as most of the thrones of western Europe toppled in the aftermath of the war.

The golden age of small suburban gardens is captured in this 1930s painting of the artist's garden by E.A.Rowe. Gertrudes Jekyll's legacy – a mixture of formal structure and informal planting – was taken up between the wars and re-interpreted in terms of the small garden, but with an emphasis on nostalgia. Seen here are elements form pre-1914 country house and cottage gardens: the sundial, containers, rustic pergola, cascades of roses and drifts of perennials.

LEFT The romantic English cottage garden has been reinterpreted in France at the Parc Floral d'Apremont, La Guerche-sur-l'Aubois, created by Gilles de Brissac from 1971 onwards. Inspired ultimately by the English cottage gardens of the Cotswolds and Surrey, by the ideas of Gertrude Jekyll and by Vita Sackville-West's garden at Sissinghurst, Apremont is a monument to the strength of this tradition, whose spell, a century on and two world wars later, still remains intact.

LEFT The revival in formality of the years before 1914 can be seen at Parnham House, Beaminster, Dorset, almost certainly laid out from 1910 by F. Inigo Thomas (1866-1950), who contributed drawings to Sir Reginald Blomfield's widely influential *The Formal Garden in England* (1892), which attacked the naturalism of William Robinson. The effect is strongly architectural, with a terrace of grass and honey-coloured paving edged with Jacobean balustrading, looking down onto a greensward with an avenue of dark green topiary cones.

Great gardens lost their creative dynamic and, where they survived, lived on only to be visited as the horticultural equivalents of state museums. To all intents and purposes they became time capsules. The future of any new large gardens henceforth lay in communal public spaces, pioneered in the previous century in municipal parks, and in the new art of landscape architecture.

The second greatest change as far as gardening was concerned, and directly related to the first, was the virtual disappearance of the gardener. The entire history of gardening until that point had been based on the assumption of the ready availability of cheap labour. Now social levelling through progressive taxation, the lure of more lucrative work in factories and the decline of the servant ethic combined to spell the end of a centuries-old tradition. Before 1914 large gardens were maintained by a small army of staff, each with a specialized skill which was passed on from one generation to the next. Even suburban gardens would normally expect the regular services of a part-time gardener, and there was always occasional semi-skilled labour to be had. After 1918 gardens and gardeners had to come to terms with these changes, and

their response was initially slow. It took time to realize that the future of the private garden was to lie in the hands of the owner-gardener.

To grasp some idea of the scale of the loss involved we need only recall that between 1900 and 1970 about a thousand country houses in Britain vanished. Statistics for losses of gardens would be far greater. All of this has contributed to what has become perhaps the single greatest factor in twentieth century-garden design: nostalgia. It had two phases. The first preceded the cataclysm, and was founded on the tradition of Victorian revivalism, but looking back this time to an idealized lost ruralism of the pre-industrial age. The second, which followed the war and as the century progressed became more obsessive, was an equally idealized yearning for the type of garden which had been at its heyday on the eve of the war. For the first of these phases we find our feet once again firmly planted in England.

The movement which was to create the legendary gardens of the years between 1890 and 1914 had its origins in a reaction against the high artifice of the mid-Victorian formal style. The key figure was William Robinson (1838-1935), two of

RIGHT The house at Le Bois des Moutiers, Varangeville-sur-Mer, France, was designed by Sir Edward Lutyens for Guillaume Mallet in 1898. The garden structure was his too, but the planting was inspired by what Mallet had seen of English gardens. Here, next to the house, a perfectly proportioned 'room' of yew with an exedra encloses box-edged beds containing a spring planting of white tulips. The idea of creating 'rooms', seen here in its infancy, was to become a dominant motif in twentieth-century garden design.

whose books were to be seminal in their influence. The first was *The Wild Garden* (1870), which set in train the revolt against Victorian formal bedding out and promoted what was to become the next century's gardening style, advocating ideas such as the naturalistic planting of drifts of bulbs in grass. The second and even more celebrated book, *The English Flower Garden* (1883), ran through fifteen editions in his own lifetime and is still in print today. This amplified his thesis in favour of a more natural style of garden design, a cause which was to be taken up by another gardening giant, Gertrude Jekyll (1843-1932), whose works are also still in print and whose position as high priestess of the garden remains unassailed even as we approach the year 2000.

To Robinson's advocacy of the natural style she added other major elements. First was a painterly theory of colour, stemming from her training as a painter and her admiration of the works of Turner. This has left a lasting mark on garden design, in the form of subtle gradations of colour within a flower border, the use of dark green yew as a background, and the evolution of planting in a single colour, for instance white, or silver and grey. Her planting was essentially nostalgic, being inspired by cottage gardens crammed with traditional herbaceous plants which cascaded beyond the confines of the border. To this she brought what she had learned from her adherence to the tenets of the Arts and Crafts Movement. This meant above all the rejection of factory-produced objects in favour of artefacts made from natural materials, especially stone and wood, and crafted in a traditional manner based on the rural vernacular style of pre-Industrial Revolution Britain. In addition to writing a long series of books covering every aspect of garden-making, she enjoyed a highly influential collaboration with the architect Sir Edwin Lutyens (1869-1944). Working together from 1893 until the outbreak of war, they produced a series of gardens

LEFT ABOVE Tintinhull, Yeovil, Somerset, created by Phyllis Reiss between the wars, is a garden directly in the Jekyll tradition, with strong structure and lush planting arranged to form a series of 'rooms', each containing a different selection of plants to unfold through the seasons. The round lily pond is a garden feature that is particularly typical of the 1920s and 30s. Here it is enclosed by dark green yew walls, which set off its exclusively white and silver planting of roses, anemones, colchicum, irises, lilies and summer hyacinths.

LEFT BELOW Hestercombe, at Cheddon Fitzpaine, Somerset, was Edwin Lutyens' and Gertrude Jekyll's masterpiece, laid out in 1904-9. Most of the original planting has now been restored, albeit in a simplified form. This picture reveals the masterly planting spaces which Lutyens' architecture provided for Miss Jekyll; and a colour combination, of purple flowers and silver-grey foliage typical of Miss Jekyll's work. (She would probably have cut off the yellow flowers.)

which epitomized the ideals of vernacular structure aligned to naturalistic planting. We should not underestimate either the importance of the advent of garden photography, which has given us records of unparalleled accuracy and detail. Between them Jekyll and Lutyens formulated the principles which, scaled down, were to dictate the design of suburban gardens of the years between the wars, with their pergolas, crazy-paving paths, stone walls with crevices stuffed with plants, sunken ponds, herbaceous borders and rose gardens. In the United States, these principles were to find their advocate in Beatrix Farrand (1872-1959).

Nostalgia for times past branched out in several directions before 1914. One expression was the revival of the sort of formality that had existed in the manor house gardens of late seventeenth-century England. Its apostle was the architect Sir Reginald Blomfield (1856-1942) whose book *The Formal Garden in England* (1892) was designed to be a counterblast to the work of William Robinson. Curiously, viewed from today's perspective, it seems to have more in common with Robinson's work than otherwise, in that both regarded good structure as essential to garden-making. To Blomfield and his followers we owe the revival both of topiary and of built features in the grand manner: terraces, summerhouses and flights of steps. In France this movement was reflected to some extent in a desire to banish the landscape style and replant gardens around the historic châteaux in the style of Le Nôtre or even earlier. Villandry, Indre-sur-Loire (1906-24), saw the creation of a great Renaissance flower garden and potager, but the work of Henri Duchêne (1841-1902) and Achille Duchêne (1866-1947), in their many restorations of historic classical gardens, was far more typical.

At the same time there was a rediscovery of the delights of the Italian Renaissance garden and a new and enthusiastic appreciation of its genius in uniting the villa with its surroundings. In America this produced a long series of Italianate gardens, including Vizcaya, Florida (1912-16) and Dumbarton Oaks, Washington D.C. (1921-47). In England its champions were Sir George Sitwell (1850-1943), who laid out Renishaw Hall (*c.* 1890), and Harold Peto (1854-1933), who designed a series of gardens in the same style. In Italy it led to the restoration of old villa gardens and to the the creation of new ones in the old manner, such as I Tatti, Florence (1909), and La Foce, Chianciano, Siena (1924-39), the work of Cecil Pinsent (1844-1939).

One of the central problems affecting garden design in this century is that the true line of descent from the past has been inherited by public spaces orchestrated by landscape architects. Today's equivalent of the country house park and the palace garden is the landscaping to be found around urban housing or along motorways, in which we can trace a response to the modernist movement in all its phases. As a result, the small private garden, however precious it may be to its owner, has become peripheral to the mainstream, showing an apparent reluctance to move forwards. Its role models and repertory remain on the whole solidly pre-1914, even though the materials and planting may have changed. This is why private gardens in this century have tended to become temples of nostalgia. One of the few designers to move the concept of the private garden on has been the American Thomas Church (1902-78), whose magnificent designs seem effortlessly to incorporate the requirements of modern living

and the swimming pool within a new vibrant style – but not one which easily crosses the Atlantic.

Small garden design has always lagged behind the grand examples, and it was not until the years between the wars that the achievements of the years before the war were assimilated. By the time this had happened – which is where this book ends – Europe was faced with another major disaster, the outbreak of the Second World War, which was to have even more far-reaching effects on every aspect of life.

Out of the two world wars and the ensuing social revolution, which brought a more equal society, emerged other problems which still affect gardening today, and for which we are still seeking a solution. The lack of labour has affected everything. It has entailed a radical retrenchment in existing gardens, the turfing over of flowerbeds, the simplification of planting, and in many cases, wholesale abondonment. Ground-cover plants have inevitably become an obsession, offering as they do maximum effect for minimum maintenance. Already by the 1920s and 30s there was a much greater emphasis on gardens consisting mostly of trees and shrubs chosen for their leaf-shape and colour, flower and berries, which called for little annual attention. The Robinsonian passion for naturalized drifts of bulbs also survived the storm. Bedding out, kitchen gardens, elaborate hedges and topiary, on the other hand, were all to fall victim to the lack of ready labour.

LEFT The painter Monet's garden at Giverny is possibly the French counterpart in terms of planting to the work of Gertrude Jekyll in England. Between 1883 and his death in 1926 the artist turned this garden into a monument to planting in the Impressionist manner, with profusion of blooms and arrangement of colour as its keynote, rather than sophistication of planting. Great stress was also laid on lifting plants upwards by means of every sort of arch and pillar, so that the visitor is enveloped in blooms. In the early-summer planting seen here a pink standard rose rises from a carpet of mixed annuals and perennials, including irises, cosmos, sweet rocket and lychnis. The gardens were restored from 1977 onwards and are only now beginning to mature, exerting as they do so a powerful influence in favour of stronger colour on current design.

RIGHT One of the herbaceous borders at The Priory, Kemerton, Hereford and Worcester, at the height of its glory in late August. Planted since the war by Peter Healing, it follows Gertrude Jekyll's principles in using a restricted range of colours. This picture shows a small section where the colour is just beginning to intensify, with pink dahlias, white Japanese anemones, Michaelmas daisies and *Sedum spectabile* just beginning to come into flower, the whole tempered by greens and an artemisia. Another of the borders follows Miss Jekyll's advice in moving from soft greys and silvers at one end through white and cream to the pinks, with the strength of colour increasing until it reaches its climax at the centre in yellows, bronzes and golds before turning softer again. Such borders are the great masterpieces of garden picture-making.

ABOVE Small ponds like this were a standard feature of gardens made between the wars, and continue to provide an attractive formula for introducing water into a garden of modest proportions. This recently constructed pool, planted with waterlilies, flag irises and grasses, is set into a verdant lawn enclosed by a shrubbery.

OPPOSITE Although this between-the-wars pond garden is, at Tintinhull, one of many different garden rooms, it offers a successful way of treating a small garden. A columned arbour looks along the central rectangular pool, whose corners are accentuated by large terracotta pots. The flanking borders are unusually planted in strongly contrasting tones, one in shades of scarlet, yellow and white, the other in soft shades of pink, mauve and blue. Dark background hedges and grey foliage plants common to both borders, unite them.

Social change was also to bring pressure to bear on the development and even the decline of the small garden. For the Victorian middle classes the garden had been not only a major status symbol but also one of the few forms of creative relaxation available to them. By 1939 the radio and the motor car were already begining to encroach on time which had formerly been spent in the garden. After 1945 gardening was almost set to begin again, but it was not until the 1970s, when some of the problems began to be solved by mechanization, that the new renaissance really took off. Ironically its ideal was not the modernist ethic, which had been present as a trickle before 1939 and found its only really major expression in the work of Thomas Church in the United States, but rather the imaginary golden age of Edwardian England.

The site is irregular, emphasizing the point that the first task in laying out a garden of this kind is to divide the site into squares, rectangles, circles and semi-circles, either radiating from the house or making vistas and cross-vistas. Slopes will need to be terraced so that each section is level, with steps in between. The lawn is 65 ft (19.8 m) at its longest, and the box parterres are each 26 ft (7.9 m) square.

THE REVIVAL OF THE FORMAL GARDEN

A feeling of timelessness and security – achieved through an abundance of built structure in gently weathered stone, geometric enclosures, stately clipped evergreens, and a profusion of old-fashioned flowers – is the key to this style of garden. The early years of the twentieth century were suffused with nostalgia: for the first time, it became fashionable to orchestrate the garden to create an optical illusion of age – akin, perhaps, to the way that reproduction furniture is distressed to make it appear antique. The intent was to evoke the gentry gardens of the seventeenth century – as the promulgators imagined them to be. It is a style complementary to that of the cottage garden which reached its apogee at about the same time, and which also viewed the past through distinctly rose-tinted spectacles.

This new return to formality differed from the earlier, Victorian, revival of formality which was basically French-inspired, hot in colour and assertively new-looking. In a broader context, it took two forms: the English manor house garden – championed by Reginald Blomfield, and the Italian Renaissance villa garden – which found particular favour in America under the aegis of Edith Wharton and Beatrix Farrand.

This design mixes elements from some of its most famous examples: Penshurst Place and Groombridge in Kent, and Athelhampton in Dorset. Although these classic English country house gardens are large, the essential ingredients can be successfully carried out on a far smaller scale. At first glance it might appear labour-intensive, but the evergreen structure requires only an annual clip, which mechanized shears will greatly facilitate, and the flower garden could be simplified by filling the beds with lavender or dwarf santolina sheared into grey mounds, which would only need replacing every five or so years. The herbaceous borders, glorious though they would be, could be slightly narrowed and filled with an avenue of standard roses bordered by lavender and underplanted with *Stachys byzantina*. But it is neither a cheap nor an instant garden. We are lucky today, however, that the manufacturers of reconstituted stone can provide, at a fraction of the cost of the stone original, a virtually complete repertory of imitations, from vases to summerhouses. Within a few years, and with a little help from an application of yoghurt, these weather to become more or less indistinguishable from the real thing. Patience is required for the yew topiary and hedges; but although it will need ten to fifteen years to reach perfection, you will be rewarded with a masterpiece, a garden whose spell is as enduring as the honey-coloured stone of its balustrade.

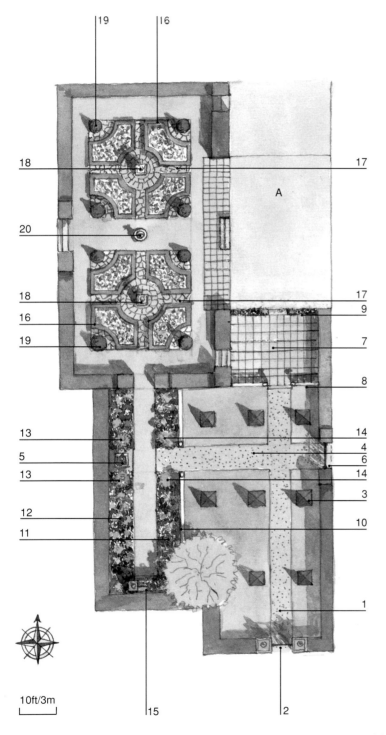

The garden is contained by yew hedges about 4 ft (1.2 m) high, with piers of 6 ft (1.8 m) giving emphasis and interest to the entrances.

THE APPROACH GARDEN
The 6 ft (1.8 m) wide gravel path (**1**) that leads from the wrought-iron gates (**2**) across the lawn and up to the stoneflagged terrace in front of the house (**A**), is flanked by yew obelisks (**3**) about 8 ft (2.4 m) high which provide a handsome vista up to the house. A second gravel path (**4**) at right angles to the approach is bounded by a lead statue (**5**) at one end and by a *claire-voyée* (a wrought-iron screen or gate to extend the view) (**6**) at the other. This type of formal arrangement of grass and clipped yews can be adapted to suit virtually any approach to the house. The yews could be cut into cones, domes or drums.

THE ENTRANCE TERRACE
This is a stone-flagged terrace (**7**) the width of the house, bounded by stone balustrades or pierced screens (**8**), and by yew hedges. Raising the terrace by two or more steps would enhance its impact immeasurably. A narrow border (**9**) against the house allows a planting to soften the severe lines; here it contains rosemary and wisteria.

THE HERBACEOUS BORDERS
Separated from the lawn by balustrades or pierced screens (**10**), the borders (**11** and **12**) are about 50 ft (15.2 m) long and 6 ft (1.8 m) wide. They are planted in the Jekyllesque manner, with substantial mounds of long-lasting grey foliage plants, such as *Senecio* 'Sunshine' and *Phlomis fruticosa*, at strategic points on either side of the statue (**13**) and the cross-axial path (**14**) giving them structure. The summerhouse (**15**) needs a climber to scramble over it: here I have suggested a quince (*Chaenomeles japonica*), a plant associated with Edwardian gardens.

THE FLOWER GARDEN
One of the essential elements of this style is a formally laid out flower garden set against a smooth lawn. Here two parterres, patterns of box-edged beds (**16**), are set within stone paving (**17**) and have statues (**18**) at their centres. Yew cones (**19**) 4 ft (1.2 m) in diameter and 6 ft (1.8 m) high provide vertical accents and contain the composition. On the grass of the central walk stands a sundial (**20**), another ornament associated with the 'old-fashioned' garden. The planting of the beds can be varied according to taste and commitment. Here we see it in spring, with yellow tulips underplanted with blue forget-me-nots. A labour-saving alternative would be to fill the beds with dwarf lavender or santolina clipped into mounds.

10ft/3m

ABOVE An alternative design for the flower garden has box-edged beds radiating out from a pool with a low fountain as the focal point. Instead of being filled with plants the water should be left clear to act as a mirror. Two pairs of yew obelisks or cones stand in the two flanking beds.Instead of block-planting, which with seasonal changes can be expensive and time-consuming, another truly authentic period piece would be a literary garden, with the beds filled with only those plants mentioned in, for example, Shakespeare's plays or Shelley's poetry. This kind of planting would necessarily be mixed and of varying heights and would make a good contrast with the tight geometrical lay-out.

LEFT The seat at the end of the walk is a typical piece of revivalist architecture and could be easily copied by using a pair of reconstituted stone gate piers and constructing the rest of preferably old brick. If you paint it all with sour milk to attract the algae, you will soon be rewarded with a suitably antique patina which can be enhanced by billowing climbers.

ABOVE A *claire-voyée* is an under-used effect in gardening. It can be a means of colonizing something attractive beyond the confines of your own garden but enhancing it by giving it the mystery of being glimpsed through lacy iron work. Here the *claire-voyée* is a gate marking the divide between the formal and informal parts of the same garden.

BELOW This woodcut from Reginald Blomfield's *The Formal Garden in England* (1892) shows exactly the type of late seventeenth-century garden which the author held up as an example to emulate and copy.

THE OLD GARDENS AT BRICKWALL NEAR NORTHIAM : SUSSEX

ABOVE Two sundials from the *c.*1910 catalogue of J.P. White's Pyghtle Works of Bedford, England, then the world's foremost suppliers of garden furniture and ornament. Both are of Portland stone and about 3 ft 6 in (1.1 m) high. Sundials based on surviving examples from the seventeenth and eighteenth centuries became an essential design feature of the 'olde worlde' garden acting as a focal point for both flower and rose garden. There is a wide range of these available in reconstituted stone today.

A TRADITIONAL COTTAGE GARDEN

The rural idyll of a cottage adrift in a sea of old-fashioned plants blooming in sweet profusion is as potent now as it was in the early years of this century when it was immortalized in a whole genre of romantic watercolour paintings. It is not surprising that so many people are attracted to this style of gardening because it seems so easy, with the plants virtually pushed in anywhere. To achieve a really painterly result, however, you need both a sure eye and a reasonable knowledge of plants.

The cult of the cottage, which overlooked the frequently dismal realities of life in the impoverished dwellings of the labouring classes, had its roots in the eighteenth century's worship of the picturesque and reached its peak towards the end of the Victorian era. The myth of the cottage garden was fostered during the last two decades of the nineteenth century by the highly influential designs and writings of William Robinson and Gertrude Jekyll, who advocated the random planting of herbaceous perennials in cottage borders. In their view cottage gardens were part of a precious heritage that had narrowly escaped extinction in the wake of the triumphant success of the mid-Victorian bedding-out style, which they now set out to topple from its pinnacle. In fact they were perfectly normal early nineteenth-century gardens, filled with the hardy perennials which nurserymen had provided for those of modest means throughout this period. The original cottage garden was therefore something quite different from our present image of it. It began as a patch for vegetables to eke out the frugal diet of the occupants, and if there were flowers at all they were there to be used: roses, lavender, sage, balm, pinks, wallflowers, jasmine, foxgloves and stocks were all grown together for medicinal purposes or to attract the bees which made the cottagers' honey. Change began to creep in in the 1860s, when the homes of the rural poor started to be prettified at the instigation of landowners. Climbers such as Virginia creeper and cultivated clematis now made their appearance, and the plant range was further extended with the inclusion of chrysanthemums, fuchsias, pelargoniums and others. By 1900 the cult of the cottage as an expression of an indigenous vernacular culture, and of cottage gardens as the ultimate expression of the 'natural' school of gardening, had become firmly enshrined in the beliefs of architects, designers and horticulturists alike. The truth is, however, that the cottage garden of our imagination is as artificial a creation as the most formal and grand of the large gardens, and those who set out to plant a cottage garden are

This minature garden is about 25 ft (7.6 m) wide and extends some 15ft (4.6 m) in front of a south-facing cottage.

not so much re-creating a lost reality as making real the rose-tinted visions of a school of watercolour painters, the most famous among them being Helen Allingham, Arthur Claude Strachan and the Stannard family.

In his immensely influential book *The English Flower Garden*, published in 1883, William Robinson wrote that one of the reasons he admired the cottage garden was that it had no plan. Though instantly recognizable as a style, it actually has no structure at all beyond the presence of an encompassing hawthorn or field hedge, picket fence or stone wall, and the principle that tall plants go at the back and small ones at the front. In the making of such a garden this has both its advantages and its disadvantages. The advantages are that cottage-gardening can be applied to virtually any shape of terrain, and that it achieves virtually instant results. The chief disadvantage is that it is labour-intensive, as it relies for its effects on the massing of herbaceous perennials, all of which require attention in the way of dividing, staking, pruning and cutting down.

Gardeners who would like something of the flavour of a cottage garden but do not relish the all-out battle to achieve it, could take a section of their garden with a southerly aspect and there make a small version. The rest of the garden could then become low-maintenance orchard and grass. My design uses a tiny area but achieves the essential effects: silhouettes of tall spikes of flowers against the wall of the house; blooms nodding over the top of the containing hedge; plants spilling over onto the path; and climbers festooning both porch and walls.

This is not a style for which it is possible to provide much in the way of ground-plans, as its inspiration is purely pictorial. It is a question more of making picturesque compositions of appropriate plants, remembering always to mass them in clumps and to encourage them to tumble over any hard surfaces. Dahlias, chrysanthemums, pelargoniums and fuchsias tended to be added as pot plants, to be brought out and dotted around in summer. These would be useful to make good any gaps in the composition as the season advances, but they do call for constant attention and watering. For devoted and patient gardeners, the *pièce de résistance* would be an example of cottage garden topiary, such as a peacock or squirrel in yew or box, to provide structural interest throughout the year. Edging the beds in box was also not unusual, and may help to give permanent structure to what can otherwise become an unruly scene.

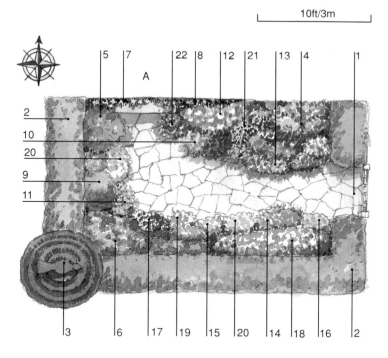

10ft/3m

Much of the garden is taken up by a rough stone path (**1**) leading to the front door of the house (**A**). The containing hedge (**2**) is of hawthorn, but a mixed field hedge is another option. This could be a marvellous opportunity to plant what is known as a 'tapestry' hedge, a mixture of holly, quickthorn and beech for example. The hedge should not be allowed to grow much over 2 ft 6 in to 3 ft (76 to 90 cm) high, to allow the sun to reach over it and to allow the plants within to rise above it. In one corner I have placed a topiary yew (**3**), which should be allowed to grow up through the hedge before being trained into a traditional shape. Remember that if you have an old yew it is never too large to be cut into shape and trained. Within as little as five years you will have a spectacular permanent garden feature requiring only an annual trim. Whether re-shaping an existing yew or starting from scratch, you need a sure hand to embark on a topiary bird; easier and almost as effective would be any variant of the tiered cake-stand. Remember to feed it with bonemeal or dried blood each spring to ensure growth. As there is only one yew in the garden, this is an occasion when I would splash out and buy a really large specimen for instant effect and start sculpting at once. The whole of the rest of the space to either side of the path is one large flowerbed, to be filled according to preference with plants from the list on page 152. It is important to include the tall plants which were always such a feature of these gardens – such as hollyhocks (**4**), sunflowers (**5**), and delphiniums (**6**). Climbers should scramble up the walls and porch: here there is a *Clematis* 'Henryi' (**7**), and a 'Paul's Himalayan Musk' rose (1848) (**8**), which is both

vigorous and graceful with open sprays of little blush-pink Noisette flowers. An alternative would be the Noisette rose 'Gloire de Dijon' (1853), an old favourite of the cottage gardens of the period when it was known as the 'Old Glory Rose'; it is buff-yellow sometimes tinted with pink and gold. An equally essential element are herbs, here represented by rosemary (*Rosmarinus officinalis*) (**9**), sage (*Salvia officinalis*) (**10**) and thyme (**11**). Fill all spaces with other old-fashioned flowers, for instance white phlox (**12**), old-fashioned pinks (**13**), old English lavender (**14**), mignonette (**15**), pansies (**16**), valerian (**17**), Madonna lilies (**18**), sweet Williams (**19**) and *Alchemilla mollis* (**20**). Remember that a cottage garden in summer would be dotted with the container plants which in winter would shelter from cold and frost on the windowsills. Here there is a purple fuchsia (**21**) and a pelargonium (**22**) both in flowerpots. A display of flowers in earthenware pots adds immeasurably to the effect but they are, of course, labour-intensive. Don't ignore the possibilities of standing them in the border to make up for perennials past their flowering period. If you grow lilies in pots they can be sunk into the bed in the containers to fill up any vacant spaces. As your garden develops, some of its most felicitous effects will be accidental through self-seeding. Foxgloves, for instance, readily self-seed and, if not moved, produce glorious spikes of purple and white. Always be prepared for such enchanting surprises by the hand of nature.

LEFT Helen Allingham's watercolours remain the ideal – to which everyone with a cottage garden aspires. Here she catches the enchantment of the style with the simple gravel path, the welcoming wicket gate and the cascades of spring bloom which include tulips, bluebells, narcissi, muscari and pansies.

BELOW A watercolour by Arthur Claude Strachan (1865-1935) encapsulates the beautiful, if labour-intensive, vision of the cottage garden. The planting is always superabundant and lush, with perennials forming a major ingredient, particularly delphiniums, phlox and hollyhocks. The foreground of the borders is always filled with low-growing, sprawling plants such as pinks and violas.

A JEKYLLESQUE GARDEN

Many of the effects that we hunger for in gardens today – a strong structure softened by planting; the use of a base colour as a backdrop and foundation to any composition; gradations of colour and the grouping of seasonal flowers in different areas of the garden – stem from the work of the greatest painter-plantswoman in garden history, Gertrude Jekyll. Her gardens, the finest of them created with the equally great architect, Sir Edwin Lutyens (1869-1944), were the supreme expressions of a golden age, the sunset years of English country buildings and gardens from 1900 to the outbreak of the First World War. While a truly authentic re-creation of one of her designs would be the work of a lifetime, it would also be a spectacle of untold delight.

For today's owner-gardener wanting to make a Jekyllesque garden, it would be difficult to take on anything beyond the broadest principles of her art, which are embodied in her book *Colour in the Flower Garden* (1908). She held that flowers which bloom at the same time should be planted close together, and above all that no colour stands alone, but only takes on its true value when considered in relation to those beside it. Thus she divided the garden into areas which would be at their peak at different times of the year, and – more important still in her view for the orchestration of a small space – she used colour with the skill and care of a painter. She produced a series of colour charts and wheels, based on the principles spelt out by the Frenchman Marcel Chevreul, which no imitator of her style should be without.

The design here is based loosely on the only small garden on which Miss Jekyll and Lutyens ever collaborated, at Millmead in Bramley, Surrey, in 1904. On a long thin site, the back garden was divided into four areas on different levels, which Lutyens articulated with the strong structure typical of his designs, including the dry-stone retaining walls of the terracing, constructed specifically to accommodate plants. A rose garden, surrounded by a shrubbery next to the house, led to a garden with a dipping well, followed by another narrowed by shrubberies to conceal utilities, and finally a small garden framing a vista of the world outside. There were no fewer than three summerhouses in this tiny space, the layout of which, together with some of the detailed planting plans, is recorded in Miss Jekyll's *Gardens for Small Country Houses* (1912). A plantswoman's paradise, it brimmed over with flowers and foliage, which engulfed the containing architecture and softened its outlines.

The garden is T-shaped, its longest extent, the east–west axis, measuring about 180 ft (54.9 m), with the lawns about 60 ft (18.3 m) long. The overall design consists of four different gardens descending from the house, and has been conceived on the Jekyll principle of assigning different seasons to the different parts of the garden: seen here is a rose garden for June; a lawn garden, basically herbaceous, for the summer months; a pergola carrying something for most seasons; a silver-grey garden for July and August; and the lawn garden leads to a fountain garden for spring and late summer flowers..

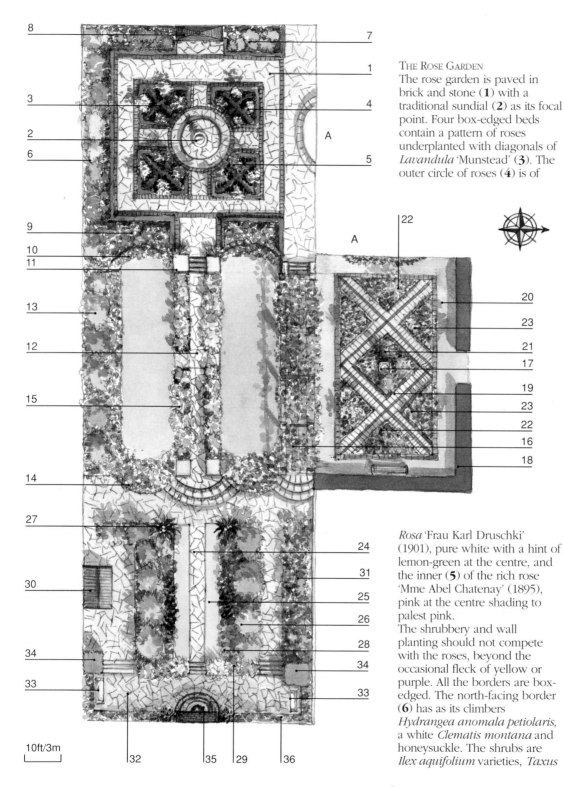

THE ROSE GARDEN

The rose garden is paved in brick and stone (**1**) with a traditional sundial (**2**) as its focal point. Four box-edged beds contain a pattern of roses underplanted with diagonals of *Lavandula* 'Munstead' (**3**). The outer circle of roses (**4**) is of *Rosa* 'Frau Karl Druschki' (1901), pure white with a hint of lemon-green at the centre, and the inner (**5**) of the rich rose 'Mme Abel Chatenay' (1895), pink at the centre shading to palest pink.

The shrubbery and wall planting should not compete with the roses, beyond the occasional fleck of yellow or purple. All the borders are box-edged. The north-facing border (**6**) has as its climbers *Hydrangea anomala petiolaris*, a white *Clematis montana* and honeysuckle. The shrubs are *Ilex aquifolium* varieties, *Taxus baccata, Mahonia aquifolium, Viburnum opulus* and white lilac. In the foreground is a mixed planting of irises, geraniums, pansies, Solomon's seal, ferns and *Helleborus orientalis*. The east-facing border (**7**) has as its climbers *Jasminum nudiflorum*, a vine and forsythia. The summerhouse (**8**) is flanked by rosemary, and the other shrubs are a mixture of *Viburnum tinus, Aucuba japonica* and elaeagnus. The west-facing box-edged beds (**9**) on the side of the curved retaining walls (**10**) are filled with plants in shades of pink, mauve and white. The piers of the steps (**11**) are flanked by prostrate rosemary, and more plants such as saxifrages, iris varieties, sedums, campanulas, pansies, hellebores, rock pinks and cerastium are tucked into crevices in the walls.

THE LAWN GARDEN

The overall composition is held together by a central stone path (**12**). The north-facing border (**13**) is planted with an evergreen screen of shrubs, and with shade-loving flowers such as hostas, tellima, violas, pulmonaria and *Tiarella cordifolia* at the front. The pink, mauve and white theme continues on the edges of this garden to tumble down the next dry-stone retaining walls (**14**) while the borders lining the central path (**15**) use blue, cream, pale yellow and silver, and are based on one part of the flowerbeds at Munstead Wood which were designed by Miss Jekyll to be at their best in high summer. Moving from the rose garden towards the fountain garden, the plants include *Crambe maritima, Iberis sempervirens, Iris pallida,*

10ft/3m

*Stachys byzantina, Eryngium ×
oliverianum*, white lilies, yellow
and white antirrhinums,
*Euphorbia characias wulfenii,
Clematis recta, Senecio bicolor
cineraria* (syn. *Cineraria
maritima), Santolina
chamaecyparissus, Bergenia
cordifolia, Campanula
lactifolia, Achillea eupatorium,
Iberis saxatilis, Ruta graveolens.*

THE PERGOLA

Pergolas were much used in
Lutyens-Jekyll gardens,
smothered with awide range
climbing plants This one (**16**) is
constructed of brick, tile and
wood, and I would suggest
planting it with a rose such as
the salmon pink 'Climbing Mme
Abel Chatenay', described by
Miss Jekyll as 'the best garden
rose in colour', honeysuckle
and *Clematis flammula.*

THE SILVER-GREY GARDEN

This is a flat garden approached
down a step from the pergola,
with a statue as its focal point
(**17**). A containing yew hedge
(**18**) acts as a foil to the plants,
which spill out from a pattern of
beds (**19**) edged in stone and
brick or tile and set in a border
of green grass (**20**). I have
suggested anchoring the
scheme with symmetrical
plantings of four *Senecio*
'Sunshine' around the statue in
the central bed (**21**), two
Phlomis fruticosa in the beds at
either end (**22**); and verbascum
in the remaining four beds (**23**).
Otherwise the beds should be
filled with a mixture of plants
with silver or grey foliage, but
be careful to choose only those
with white or yellow flowers:
white 'Mrs Sinkins' pinks,
white lychnis, *Senecio bicolor
cineraria*, ballota and santolina
would all be possible. A *Cytisus
battandieri* climbs against the
wall of the house (**A**).

THE FOUNTAIN GARDEN

Returning to the main garden
the last terrace narrows the
garden's perspective and gives
it a feeling of increased length.
The path (**24**) is flanked by
grass (**25**) and two shrub
borders (**26**) planted with
evergreens bearing small
flowers and berries – eucryphia,
osmanthus, *Ilex aquifolium*,
mahonia and skimmia. These
are underplanted with spring
bulbs and flowers: snowdrops,
narcissi, fritillaries, *Iris
reticulata*, sternbergia, gentians
and hellebores; hostas and lilies
provide later interest. The ends
of the borders are held by
evergreen 'full stops' – yuccas
(**27**) and bergenia (**28**). At the
end, opposite the fountain, is a
summer border (**29**) in blue and
white containing, for example,
delphiniums, gypsophila,
potentillas and *Centaurea
montana*. To one side the shrub
border conceals a garden shed
(**30**), and to the other it follows
a path along a south-facing
border (**31**) of Michaelmas
daisies offset with white-
flowering climbers:*Clematis
montana* and *Rosa* 'Mme Alfred
Carrière' (1879), regarded by
Miss Jekyll as 'the best white
climbing rose'. The cross-axis
path (**32**) at the end of the
garden terminates each side
with a seat (**33**) hedged in by
clipped Portugal laurel (**34**).
The wall fountain (**35**) is a
simple built structure (see page
1). The walls are clothed with
climbers planted in the narrow
beds (**36**): ceanothus, ivy,
jasmine and a pink
chaenomeles; these are
underplanted with swathes of
bergenia. I would plant a
cotoneaster over the north-
facing seat and a passionflower
over the south-facing one.

ABOVE An autochrome photograph taken by Miss Jekyll in the 1900s of a
section of the grey, white, blue and pink border in her garden at Munstead
Wood. The careful combination of graduated colour, of plants in ascending
clumps from a strong baseline planting, are the hallmarks of her style.
BELOW A brick and wood pergola designed by Percy Cane (1881-1976) in
the 1920s for a garden at Kingswood House, Sunningdale, Surrey. The
pergola became ubiquitous by 1914, a gracious architectural support
designed in response to the massive expansion in varieties of climbers other
than roses. Pergolas could be as solid as this one or a simple construction of
larch poles.

A POST-WAR SUBURBAN GARDEN

This type of garden represents the golden age of middle-class gardening. It speaks of enthusiasm and commitment: those who make or restore one will never want to leave it. The huge popularity of the style – which maintains to this day – owes much to the format it offers for small sites: its division into geometric areas means that elements can be dropped or rearranged according to taste and available space. There is only one fixed point: the lawn, which is sacrosanct.

Between 1920 and before cheap garden labour vanished in 1939, the cult of the vernacular and the late Victorian revival of formality combined to create a type of small garden ideally suited to middle-class family houses in the suburbs. They followed a similar pattern, and their ingredients were constant though shifting: they were formal in style, with a fence, wall or hedge dividing the fruit and vegetable garden from the garden proper; the pleasure garden was then further divided by trellises and hedges in order to incorporate a number of pre-ordained elements.

Of these the lawn was the most important, assuming a position of pre-eminence that has remained immutable ever since. Paths never traversed its unbroken green expanse but were always placed to one side. The sanctity of the lawn reflected a period which cultivated the outdoors. The garden, as a consequence of the belief in the beneficial effects of the sun, was deliberately designed to catch its rays in the large central spaces devised to accomodate the proliferation of portable garden furniture – above all the ubiquitous deck chair – and to allow children to play.

Among other elements of the style, the favourite was the rose garden, owing to the advent of the Hybrid Teas which flowered repeatedly over a long season. Also popular were flower gardens, especially those containing 'old-fashioned' flowers and herbaceous borders, and few of these gardens were devoid of water, even if only a small pool. Occasionally, too, there would be a herb garden or rockery.

Great emphasis was given to ground patterns, with paths and paved areas in brick and stone, and crazy paving in huge quantities. Garden buildings were rare, and the most frequent garden ornament was a sundial; birdbaths also proliferated, while statuary shrank in scale. Many of the typical features of this style are included in my design which is adapted from one in George Dillistone's *The Planning and Planting of Little Gardens* (1920), one of the numerous books recording garden designs of the period.

The garden is L-shaped, about 150 x 100 x 50 ft (45.7 x 30.5 x 15.2 m), and within this the space is firmly divided by means of trellis and hedges. The pond is in the north-west corner of the garden. The garden is surrounded by a wooden fence about 5 ft (1.5 m) high, which is topped by trellis in the pleasure garden in order to accommodate climbers and ensure privacy.

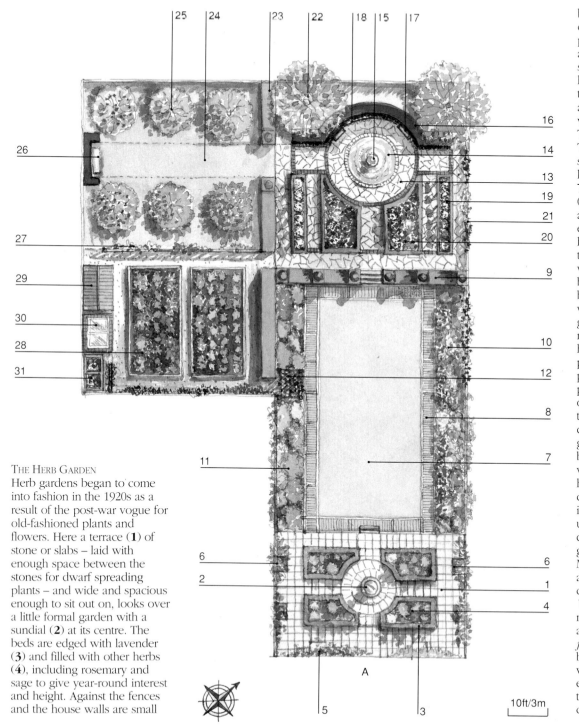

beds (**5** and **6**) for climbers: a clematis, perhaps the cyclamen pink 'Comtesse de Bouchaud', and a passionflower on the south-facing wall, climbing hydrangea and jasmine against the house, and Virginia creeper and pyracantha on the north-west facing fence.

THE LAWN GARDEN

The lawn garden is slightly sunken, and its focus is a well-kept lawn (**7**), 56 x 26 ft (17.1 x 7.9 m), surrounded by a path (**8**) of patterned brick and stone about 3 ft (90 cm) wide. At one end it is bounded by a yew hedge (**9**), cut into shapes typical of the period hedge, which conceals the rose garden beyond but affords a glimpse between its piers of the fountain which is the focus of the garden's main axis. Yew remains by far the best plant for hedging, although it calls for patience, but thuja or golden privet would be equally good period alternatives. Another option would be decorative trelliswork covered with climbing roses. The lawn garden is flanked by two borders. The one with the warm, southerly aspect (**10**) is herbaceous, and will need careful planning to ensure that it is constantly in bloom from May until October. Here it is depicted in its late autumn glory, with a display of Michaelmas daisies, heleniums and helianthus. There are climbers behind, including a *Vitis coignetiae* for its marvellous autumn colouring and violet-purple *Clematis × jackmanii*. The north-facing border (**11**) is filled in the main with shrubs chosen for their evergreen or variegated foliage, their flowers or their fruits: cotoneasters, cytisus, yellow-

THE HERB GARDEN

Herb gardens began to come into fashion in the 1920s as a result of the post-war vogue for old-fashioned plants and flowers. Here a terrace (**1**) of stone or slabs – laid with enough space between the stones for dwarf spreading plants – and wide and spacious enough to sit out on, looks over a little formal garden with a sundial (**2**) at its centre. The beds are edged with lavender (**3**) and filled with other herbs (**4**), including rosemary and sage to give year-round interest and height. Against the fences and the house walls are small

10ft/3m

A

edged elaeagnus, laurustinus, purple berberis, *Aucuba japonica*, cornus and deutzia. The front of the border is underplanted with spring bulbs, and the trellis behind is covered with forsythia and honeysuckle. Halfway along the border is a trellis arch (**12**) spanning a slope for wheelbarrow access to the kitchen garden. Plant a rose over the arch, perhaps the pink 'Dorothy Perkins' (1902).

THE ROSE GARDEN

Two or three steps lead up to the rose garden, which is paved with stone and brick in geometric patterns (**13**). Its focal point is a pond (**14**), 12 ft (3.6 m) in diameter, with water lilies, which were enormously popular at this period, surrounding a central fountain (**15**). This is silhouetted against a yew exedra 6 ft (1.8 m) high (**16**), which also conceals the boundary fence. An alternative to the yew would be to build a brick and rendered wall, with flanking piers and coping, to make the same shape; this would allow you to grow more climbers. Within the exedra's curve are two wooden seats (**17**), and a narrow bed (**18**) of *Viola riviniana purpurea* (formerly known as *V. labradorica purpurea*). The rose beds here are edged with box and filled with red and white roses. Another colour scheme could be chosen from the considerable number of roses of the period 1900-39 which are still available today. The two long flanking beds (**19**) are filled with a line of standard 'Little White Pet' roses (1879), underplanted with lavender-coloured violas. The two central beds (**20**) are filled with Hybrid Tea roses in the strong colours favoured in the period: *RR.*

'Gustav Grünerwald' (1903), 'Marchioness of Salisbury' (1890), 'Reverend F. Page-Roberts' (1921), 'Shot Silk' (1914) and 'W.E. Lippiat' (1907). The underplanting here is of deep purple violas. On the south-facing fence (**21**) are two red Hybrid Tea climbers, 'Climbing General MacArthur' (1923) and 'Souvenir de Claudius Denoyel' (1920), flanking the white Hybrid Perpetual 'Frau Karl Druschki' (1906). Behind the exedra is grass, planted with two flowering cherries (**22**): varieties with pink blossom and bronze leaves would be correct for the period. A golden privet hedge (**23**) divides the decorative from the productive gardens.

THE ORCHARD

The orchard has a mown-grass walk (**24**) leading through rough-cut grass and an avenue of fruit trees (**25**) (perhaps two pears, two apples and two plums) to a wooden seat set in a clipped yew niche (**26**). The grass should be wild-planted with narcissi for spring.

THE KITCHEN GARDEN

The kitchen garden is divided from the orchard by a trellis fence (**27**) which could be used to support climbers. It has enough space for vegetables and fruit bushes (**28**), a toolshed (**29**), cold frame (**30**) and compost heaps (**31**) hidden by a trellis or fence. Today when a huge range of fresh fruit and vegetables is readily available in stores, we tend to forget the importance of the role played by a productive kitchen garden. If, however, such a garden is superfluous to your needs, you could easily extend the orchard, or re-site the herb garden away from the house and extend the lawn and herbaceous borders.

ABOVE An autumnal herbaceous border painted by Lilian Stannard between the wars is Jekyllesque in its profusion if not in its colour control for here we see red and yellow juxtaposed.. The path, in crazy paving edged with brick and with a swathe of grass to offset the border each side, leads to a vine-covered arbour.

LEFT A post-Jekyll rose garden very different from its Victorian predecessor. It is hedged with dark green yew to set off the flowers to supreme advantage and given strong ground pattern by the herringbone brick paths.

A POST-WAR SUNKEN GARDEN

The appeal of this type of design to those making gardens in the prosperous suburbs in the 1920s and 30s was huge and still retains its fascination today. It is one of the few new formats able to give a logical and elegant change of level, however modest, to small sites. As a successful solution for incorporating water in the small garden it remains unbeaten, principally because it uses water in an unashamedly architectural manner and never masquerades as artificial nature.

Although the sunken garden had its origins in elements of the pre-First World War gardening style, it became so typical as to be almost the hallmark of the post-war period. The revival of formality, an interest in water and water plants and the Jekyllesque delight in softening built structure with sprawling, low-growing plants had all been striking features of the pre-war period. Apart from fountains, water in particular had not been a feature of the small Victorian garden but, as the new century progressed, the delights of water became progressively more accessible to gardeners working on even the smallest of sites, thanks to inexpensive methods of construction and more recently to the introduction of electric pumps. Sunken gardens became a reflection of the obsession with sunlight which marked the years between the wars, expressed in the new-fangled cult of sunbathing and the sunburst motif which permeated the Art Deco style.

One of the earliest sunken gardens was designed by H. Inigo Triggs (1876-1923), a great advocate of formality, at Little Boarhunt, Liphook, Hampshire. It contains all the elements which were to be repeated until the formula became a cliché: a sunken rectangle of grass focusing on a geometrically articulated sheet of water, short flights of steps down, and rock plants trailing over the enclosing walls.

The design here is based on one of the many given in G.C. Taylor's *The Modern Garden* (1936) which rework the formula with endless variations on the number of flights of steps and the use of more or less paving and built features. Usually the sunken garden was also contained, as here, by a generous herbaceous border, or sometimes two.

This is not a demanding garden, and the workload could be further reduced by paving the central area and leaving crevices for plants. Once established, these will look after themselves. The main expenditure involved would be on the construction. As this is a typically flat garden, care should be taken to introduce some permanent vertical accents, preferably in the form of evergreens, as otherwise it could look dull.

The sunken area is 40 x 25 ft (12.2 x 7.6 m). Whichever way it faces it must be positioned in the open, with no surrounding or overhanging shrubs or trees, so that the light can play on the pond and plants, and the sky and sun can be reflected in its waters. The area is sunk by some 3 ft (90 cm) and the pond, which is shallow, measures 18 x 9 ft (5.5 x 2.7 m).

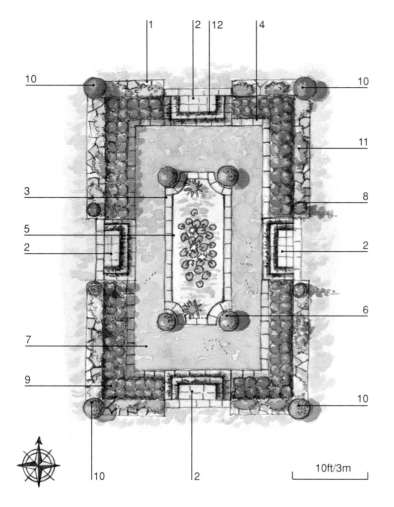

10ft/3m

Any clipped evergreens would be as appropriate. If the containers were portable and you had enough space to store them elsewhere in your garden you could, with careful planning, have a succession of bloom here all through the year. One of the joys of water is looking at it — both for the flowers of its plants and for the reflections of changing light. A comfortable seat could be sited at the top of any of the flight of steps leading down to the pond. If you do this, you might replace the topiary spirals with a planting of rosemary or lavender . The beds (**9**) are planted with *Lavandula* 'Hidcote', which has beautiful deep purple flower spikes at the height of summer and attractive grey foliage throughout the year. Catmint (nepeta) would be an alternative, but whatever the choice it should be planted in blocks in order to offset the spotty, haphazard growth of the rock plants. Although this is essentially a summer garden, there could with care be a spring planting of white tulips. The surrounding paving and walls are given formal punctuation marks at the corners by a repetition of the box balls (**10**). In small spaces at the top of the wall (**11**) and in the crevices is a planting of white snow-in-summer (*Cerastium tomentosum*) and purple aubrieta; purple thyme and white arabis or *Iberis saxatilis* could be substituted or added. Arenaria (**12**) is growing between the slabs of the steps, but thyme would do as well. Clearly the garden could accommodate any number of colour schemes. Pink and white would be a pretty alternative, perhaps with saxifrages in the

crevices and dianthus in the beds, as would a planting based entirely on silver and grey foliage plants. Planting in any surrounding border should echo the theme. The illustration on the previous page includes *Stachys byzantina*, white iris, verbascum, *Geranium macrorrhizum album*, *Dianthus* 'Mrs Sinkins', two of the small conifers that were fashionable at the time – *Thuja occidentalis* and *T. orientalis* 'Marrison Sulphur' – and *Picea glauca* 'Alberta Globe'.

BELOW An alternative design has a circular pool large enough to accommodate water plants and a low single jet at its centre. The paving is a mixture of crazy paving around the pool, with brick and rectangular stone or slabs for the paths. Four areas of grass lead to the encompassing flowerbed, which would be both handsome and period filled with silver and gold plants such as *Senecio* 'Sunshine', *Artemisia arborescens*, *Phlomis fruticosa*, *Stachys byzantina* and ballota. The wall crevices could be planted with creeping arabis, *Alchemilla mollis* and *Cerastium tomentosum*.

The paving (**1**) that surrounds the sunken area is in the crazy paving style of the 1920s and 30s, though stone or slabs would be good alternatives. The steps (**2**), the pond (**3**) and its surrounding flowerbeds (**4**) are edged with the same materials cut to shape. Another option would be to edge the pool and beds with brick which matches that in the retaining wall. A small statue in the whimsical vein of the period could be an attractive feature in the middle of the pond. The garden is planted exclusively in purple and white. The pond (**5**) contains white water lilies,

some varieties of which will thrive in as little as a foot (30 cm) of water, and clumps of hardy marginal aquatics chosen from the wide range available, including purple *Iris versicolor*. At the corners are four clipped box balls (**6**) to give year-round interest. There could be any amount of variation here, with sentinels of Irish yew, for instance, or containers to allow seasonal planting. The pond is surrounded by lawn (**7**), but the whole area could instead be paved, with crevices left for plants. At the descents, ivy trained in spirals in earthenware containers (**8**) act as sentinels.

LEFT Colour reproduction was just coming in during the 1930s, giving us new and better information on the actual appearance of gardens. This photograph, from Richard Sudell's *Landscape Gardening* (1933), captures the great interest in sprawling rock plants tucked between the crevices of the newly fashionable crazy paving.

BELOW Design by Jean S. Houchin for a small pond garden from Percy Cane's *Garden Design* (1931) There are steps down and a seat in one corner. The pond is surrounded by a mixed planting in the main in grey, blue and purple, including *Stachys byzantina*, delphiniums, lupins, Canterbury bells and nepeta.

BELOW This sunken garden in Ardmore, Pennsylvania, *c.*1925 is a typically geometric one, with stepped stone coping. Ponds like this became enormously popular at that time, and were almost always sited well clear of large trees in order to catch the sun.

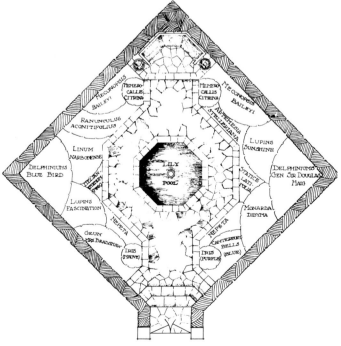

PLANTS FOR PERIOD GARDENS

Almost all the plants in the following lists are available from nurseries in the British Isles. However, many of the old tulip varieties are only found in specialist collections in Holland.

The lists do not duplicate plants recommended in the text, nor those suitable for earlier styles of garden. In general, any of the plants listed for earlier gardens would still be available for use in gardens of a later date and style. Thus, for a late Victorian garden, any of the plants recommended for older gardens could be used; indeed some of them would have been just as popular in Victorian times as they were when first introduced.

Such popular plants generally quickly found their way around the gardens and nurseries of North America and Europe. The lists therefore apply equally there and, with only a few exceptions, the key plants listed would have been available throughout these areas.

Common names are given when the plants were better known by these names, or when the Latin identification is uncertain.

A LATE MEDIEVAL GARDEN 1450–1500

Flowery Mead
cinquefoil (*Potentilla* spp.)
clover (*Trifolium pratense*)
columbine (*Aquilegia vulgaris*)
cowslip (*Primula veris*)
field scabious (*Knautia arvensis*)
meadow sage (*Salvia pratensis*)
meadowsweet (*Filipendula vulgaris*)
poppy (*Papaver rhoeas*)
primrose (*Primula vulgaris*)
selfheal (*Prunella vulgaris*)
stavesacre (*Delphinium staphisagria*)
tansy (*Tanacetum vulgare*)
yarrow (*Achillea millefolium*)

Raised Beds
artichoke, globe
balm (*Melissa officinalis*)
basil
bay
black hellebore (*Helleborus niger*)
borage
chives
dragons (*Dracunculus vulgaris*)
feverfew
great celandine (*Chelidonium majus*)
hollyhock
hyssop
Iris 'Florentina', *I. germanica* & *I. pseudacorus*
lovage
mint
monkshood (*Aconitum napellus*)
parsley
origano
peony (*Paeonia mascula* & *P. officinalis*)
periwinkle

rue
sage
savory (*Satureja hortensis*)
sea holly (*Eryngium maritimum*)
Solomon's seal (*Polygonatum multiflorum*)
southernwood
wallflower
sweet rocket

Fruit Trees
almond
apples: 'Coeur de Boeuf', 'Costard', 'Decio', Nonpareil' & 'Pearmain'
bullace, black
damson
myrobalan or cherry plum, yellow plum 'Mirabelle de Nancy' & 'White Magnum Bonum'
walnut

AN ITALIAN RENAISSANCE GARDEN 1550–1600

Bosco
Arbutus unedo (strawberry tree)
Celtis australis
Ceratonia siliqua (carob)
Cercis siliquastrum (Judas tree)
Colutea arborescens (bladder senna)
Cornus mas (cornelian cherry)
Fraxinus ornus (manna ash)
Hibiscus syriacus
Laburnum alpinum
Laurus nobilis (sweet bay)
Melia azedarach
Morus alba (white mulberry)
Paliurus spina-christi (Christ's thorn)
Philadelphus coronarius
Phillyrea angustifolia & *P. latifolia*

Pinus pinea (stone or umbrella pine)
Pistacia lentiscus (mastic) & *P. terebinthus* (terebinth)
Quercus suber (cork oak)
Rhus cotinus (Venetian sumach)
Ruscus hypoglossum
Spartium junceum (Spanish broom)
Staphylea pinnata (bladder nut)
Styrax officinalis (storax)
Tamarix gallica
Vitex agnus-castus (chaste tree)

Orchard
apple 'Api Rose', 'Chataignier', 'Francatu' & 'Haut Bonté'
apricot (*Prunus armeniaca*)
azarole (*Crataegus azarolus*)
cherry (*Prunus avium* & *P. cerasus*)
olive (*Olea europaea*)
persimmon (*Diospyros lotus*)
pistachio (*Pistacia vera*)
service tree (*Sorbus domestica*)
vine (*Vitis vinifera* e.g. 'Schiava Grossa' (= 'Black Hamburgh'))

Pots
Agave americana
Capsicum annuum (winter cherry)
Dianthus caryophyllus (carnation)
Ficus carica (fig)
Nerium oleander (oleander)
Yucca gloriosa

Orto
Acanthus mollis
Anemone coronaria & *A. hortensis*
Anthemis tinctoria
Antirrhinum majus (snapdragon)
Asphodeline lutea
Aster amellus
Calamintha grandiflora

Campanula medium (Canterbury bells), *C. persicifolia* & *C. glomerata*
Celosia cristata
Centaurea cyanea & *C. montana*
Chamaemelum nobile 'Plenum' (double camomile)
Convallaria majalis (lily-of-the-valley)
Cyclamen purpurascens
Dianthus barbatus (sweet William) & *D. deltoides*
Dictamnus albus
Fritillaria imperialis (crown imperial) & *F. persica*
Gladiolus communis
Hemerocallis lilio-asphodelus
Hermodactylus tuberosus (snake's head iris)
Hyacinthus orientalis
Narcissus tazetta
Iris variegata
Lavandula stoechas (French lavender)
Leucojum vernum
Lilium bulbiferum & *L. martagon*
Lunaria annua (honesty)
Lychnis coronaria
Malva moschata
Matthiola incana (stock)
Muscari botryoides (grape hyacinth)
Narcissus poeticus
Nigella damascena (love-in-a-mist)
Paeonia officinalis 'Rubra Plena'
Pancratium maritimum
Papaver somniferum
Physalis alkekengi
Ranunculus asiaticus
Salvia sclarea
Satureja montana
Tagetes patula (French marigold)
Tulipa schrenkii
Veratrum album

Viola odorata double
Viscaria alpina
Xeranthemum annuum

A NORTHERN RENAISSANCE GARDEN 1580 –1630

Potager

asparagus, beetroot, broad bean, cabbage, chicory, carrot, gooseberry, kale, leek, lettuce, onion, parsnip, pea, pumpkin, potato, radish, redcurrant, strawberry (*Fragaria vesca*), turnip

Orchard

apple 'Calville Blanc d'Hiver', 'Calville Rouge d'Hiver', 'Court Pendu Plat', 'Fenouillet Gris', 'London Pippin', 'Royal Russet' & 'Scarlet Crofton'
bullace, white
cherry 'Morello' & 'Noble' (syn. 'Tradescant's Heart')
damson, common
myrobalan or cherry plum, red
pear 'Bishop's Thumb', 'Black Worcester' & 'Windsor'
plum 'Green Gage' ('Verdoch' of Parkinson) & 'Red Magnum Bonum'

Flower Garden – Bulbs, Corms & Tubers

Allium moly
Crocus susianus & *C. vernus*
Cyclamen hederifolium
Eranthis hyemalis
Erythronium dens-canis
Fritillaria pyrenaica
Iris xiphioides (English iris) & *I. xiphium* (Spanish i.)
Leucojum aestivum
Lilium chalcedonicum
Muscari comosum, M. c. 'Plumosum' & *M. muscarimi*
Narcissus 'Eystettensis' (Queen Double Daffodil, after Anne of Denmark, queen consort of James I & VI), *N. jonquilla* & *N. poeticus, N.* 'Telamonius Plenus' (syn. 'Van Sion')

Scilla peruviana
Sternbergia lutea
Tulipa gesneriana

Flower Garden – Annual, Biennial & Herbaceous Flowers

Amaranthus caudatus
Anaphalis margaritacea
Anemone sylvestris
Anthericum liliago
Astrantia major
Ballota pseudodictamnus
Campanula pyramidalis
Catananche caerulea
Centranthus ruber
Consolida ajacis (larkspur)
Digitalis lutea
Echinops ritro & *E. sphaerocephalus*
Galega officinalis
Gentiana acaulis & *G. lutea*
Geranium macrorrhizum
Helianthus annuus (sunflower)
Hemerocallis fulva
Hepatica triloba (including double blue & double deep pink)
Hesperis matronalis (sweet rocket) double forms
Hibiscus trionum
Iberis umbellata (candytuft)
Iris graminea, I. pumila & *I. sibirica*
Lunaria rediviva
Lychnis chalcedonica
Primula auricula
Ranunculus acris 'Flore Pleno' & *R. aconitifolius* 'Flore Pleno' (both known as Buttons or Bachelor's Buttons)
Tagetes erecta (African marigold)
Veratrum album & *V. nigrum*

Climbers for Pergola

Clematis cirrhosa & *C. viticella*
Jasminum officinale
Lonicera periclymenum
Vitis labrusca & *V. vinifera* e.g. 'Pinot Meunier'

A FRENCH CLASSICAL GARDEN 1650 –1700

Wall Plants – Fruit

apple 'Calville Rouge d'Automne', 'Fenouillet Rouge', 'Golden Reinette', 'Margaret', 'Pigeon de Jérusalem' & 'Reinette de Macon'
cherry 'May Duke'
pear 'Bon Chrétien d'Hiver', 'Martin Sec' & 'Virgouleuse'
plum 'Blue Perdrigon', 'D'Agen' (syn. 'D'Ente'), 'Mirabelle de Metz' & 'Orléans'

Wall Plants – Climbers

Campsis radicans
Lonicera sempervirens
Vitis labrusca

Border Plants – Bulbs, Corms & Tubers

Crocus biflorus
Cyclamen repandum
Erythronium americanum
Iris persica
Lilium pomponium
Narcissus bulbocodium, N. minor, N. pseudonarcissus moschatus, N. × odorus & *N. triandrus*
Tulipa clusiana

Border plants – Annuals, Biennials & Herbaceous

Acanthus spinosus
Achillea taygetea
Adonis aestivalis
Ajuga genevensis
Amberboa moschata (sweet sultan)
Aquilegia canadensis
Artemisia arborescens
Aruncus dioicus
Bassia scoparia (syn. *Kochia s.*)
Centaurea rhapontica
Cerastium tomentosum
Convolvulus tricolor
Cynara cardunculus (cardoon)
Eryngium amethystinum
Eupatorium purpureum
Gentiana asclepiadea
Heuchera americana
Iberis semperflorens
Iris × sambucina
Linaria purpurea

Lobelia cardinalis & *L. syphilitica*
Nigella hispanica
Oenothera biennis
Omphalodes linifolia & *O.verna*
Paeonia peregrina
Paradisea liliastrum
Physostegia virginiana
Potentilla recta
Poterium canadense
Pulsatilla alpina
Rudbeckia laciniata
Salvia verticillata
Sanguinaria canadensis
Santolina pinnata neapolitana
Scabiosa atropurpurea & *S. graminifolia*
Senecio cineraria
Smilacina racemosa
Tradescantia virginiana double blue *Yucca filamentosa*

A 'WILLIAM AND MARY' GARDEN 1680 –1720

Bulbs, Corms & Tubers

Amaryllis belladonna
Colchicum agrippinum, C. byzantinum & *C. autumnale* 'Pleniflorum'
Crocus flavus, C. angustifolius & *C. × stellaris*
Cyclamen coum & *C. purpurascens*
Dactylorhiza maculata & *D. majalis*
Fritillaria imperialis 'Aureomarginata', 'Duplex', 'Flava', 'Lutea' & 'Rubra Maxima'
Galanthus nivalis
Hyacinthoides hispanica
Lilium candidum 'Plenum'
Muscari macrocarpum
Narcissus jonquilla 'Plena' & *N. poeticus* 'Plenus '
Nerine sarniensis
Ornithogalum nutans & *O. umbellatum*
Tulipa cvs. ('Amiral de Constantinople', 'Dido', 'Duc van Tol', 'Gala Beauty', 'Lac van Rijn', 'Lutea Major', 'Paragon Everwijn', 'Semper Augustus' & 'Zomerschoon')

Annual Biennial & Herbaceous Flowers

Agapanthus africanus
Aquilegia vulgaris clematiflora
Aster tradescantii
Bellis perennis 'Parkinson's Great White' & 'Prolifera' (hen & chickens daisy)
Calendula officinalis 'Prolifera'
Centranthus ruber albus
Clematis viticella 'Purpurea Plena Elegans'
Dianthus cvs. ('Argus', 'Fenbow Nutmeg Clove', *gratiano-politanus* 'Double Cheddar', 'Old Dutch Pink', 'Old Fringed Pink', 'Old Fringed White', 'Painted Lady', 'Pheasant's Eye', 'Queen of Sheba' & 'Sops in Wine')
Digitalis purpurea alba
Euphorbia cyparissias
Fragaria vesca 'Muricata' (Plymouth strawberry)
Geranium pratense albiflorum, G. sanguineum striatum & *G. sylvaticum*
Helleborus argutifolius
Impatiens balsamina
Ipomoea nil
Iris spuria
Lathyrus latifolius
Lobularia maritima (alyssum)
Lupinus angustifolius
Lychnis chalcedonica 'Plena', *L. coronaria alba* & *L. flos-cuculi* 'Plena'
Matthiola incana double
Nigella damascena blue, purple & double
Physalis alkekengi
Primula × *pubescens* & *P. vulgaris* double yellow
Tanacetum parthenium double
Verbascum phoeniceum

Orchard

apple 'Bridgwater Pippin', 'Colonel Vaughan', 'Devonshire Quarrenden', 'Flower of Kent', 'Golden Harvey' & 'Lemon Pippin'
cherry 'Carnation' & 'Gascoigne'
damson 'Prune Damson'

pear 'Chaumontel', 'Uvedale's St Germain' & (perry) 'Barland'
plum 'Catalonia', 'Early Orleans' & 'German Prune'

AN EARLY NEW ENGLAND GARDEN 1690–1780

Front Garden

Argemone grandiflora
Callistephus chinensis (China aster)
Chelone glabra
Coreopsis lanceolata
Galax urceolata
Galium verum (yellow bedstraw)
Geranium maculatum
Hibiscus moscheutos (rose mallow)
Iris cristata
Lathyrus odoratus (sweet pea) old cvs. e.g. 'Matucana', 'Painted Lady'
Lychnis viscaria
Lysimachia nummularia
Mertensia virginica
Monarda didyma
Phlox divaricata, P. glaberrima, P. maculata & *P. paniculata*
Pulmonaria augustifolia
Ranunculus creticus
Rudbeckia hirta
Silene dioica
Stokesia laevis
Tiarella cordifolia
Veronica longifolia
Viola canadensis, V. obliqua, V. pedata, V. sororia & *V. striata*

Vegetables

beans (kidney, lima, Carolina, scarlet runner), black-eyed pea, broccoli, cayenne pepper, celery, corn (Indian or sweet), lentil, marrow, melon, okra, squash, sweet potato, tobacco, yam

A GEORGIAN TOWN GARDEN 1730–1780

Flowers

Armeria maritima (thrift – for edgings)
Asclepias syriaca & *A. tuberosa*
Aster dumosus, A. novae-angliae, A. novi-belgii & *A. sedifolius* (Michaelmas daisies)
Campanula pyramidalis & *C. trachelium* double blue & double white
Cheiranthus cheiri 'Bloody Warrior' & 'Harpur Crewe' (a Victorian name for a much older plant)
Coreopsis lanceolata
Dianthus chinensis (Indian pink)
Digitalis ferruginea
Echinacea purpurea (coneflower)
Glaucium flavum (horned poppy)
Gomphrena globosa (globe amaranth)
Hedysarum coccineum & *H. c. album* (red & white French honeysuckle)
Helenium autumnale
Kniphofia uvaria
Malcolmia incana (Brompton stock & ten week double stock) & *M. maritima* (Virginia stock)
Medicago intertexta (hedgehogs) & *M. scutellata* (snails)
Nepeta mussinii (catmint)
Papaver orientale (oriental poppy)
Polygonatum odoratum 'Flore Pleno' (double Solomon's seal)
Reseda odorata (mignonette)
Salvia viridis (clary)
Saxifraga granulata 'Flore Pleno'
Scorpiurus vermiculatus
Solidago (golden rod)
Tulipa cvs. ('Blue Flag', 'Claermond Silver', 'Cramoisi', 'Duc van Tol Aurora' (also other 'Duc van Tol' sports including Cochineal, Max Cramoisi, Orange, Rose, Salmon, Violet), 'Keizerskroon','Marquis', 'Paeony Gold', 'Paeony Red', 'Perfecta', 'Viceroy', 'Wapen van Leiden' & 'Waarschijnlijk Paeony Gold')
Vinca major & *V. minor*

Fruit

apple cvs. ('Ashmead's Kernel', 'Blenheim Orange', 'Margil', 'Orange Pippin', 'Ribston Pippin' & Wheeler's Russet')
cherry 'Belle de Choisy'
pear cvs. ('Autumn Bergamot', Rance', 'Citron des Carmes', 'Jargonelle', 'Marquise' & 'Passe Colmar')

AN EARLY LANDSCAPE GARDEN 1720–1750

Trees & Shrubs

The designs and garden accounts by the Reverend Joseph Spence mention common names which most probably refer to the species below.

Abies alba (silver fir)
Acer platanoides (Norway or Swedish maple), *A. saccharinum* (Sir Charles Wager's maple)
Arbutus andrachne
Artemisia abrotanum (southernwood)
Cedrus libani (cedar of Lebanon)
Colutea arborescens (bladder senna)
Corylus colurna (Turkish hazel) & *C. maxima* (filbert)
Crataeaus laevigata & *C monogyna* (may)
Cydonia oblonga (quince)
Cytisus scoparius (common broom)
Daphne mezereum & *D. m. alba*
Juniperus virginiana (Virginia cedar)
Magnolia grandiflora
Philadelphus coronarius (syringa or mock orange)
Picea abies (Norway spruce)
Pinus pinaster (cluster pine) & *P. strobus* (Weymouth pine)
Populus alba (abele), *P. nigra* (black poplar), *P. tacamahaca* (Carolinian or balsam poplar) & *P. tremula* (aspen)
Prunus avium (wild cherry), *P. avium* 'Flore Pleno' (double

gean), *P. glandulosa* 'Rosea Plena', *P. persica* double flowered (d. f. peach) & *P. virginiana* (Virginian bird cherry)

Quercus coccinea (scarlet oak) & *Q. rubra* (red oak)

Rosa × centifolia (Provence or cabbage rose), *R. eglanteria* (sweet briar), *R. foetida* (single yellow rose), *R. gallica* (Provins rose) & *R. g.* 'Versicolor' (Rosa Mundi)

Salix alba vitellina (Dutch yellow-rind willow) & *S. babylonica* (weeping willow)

Spartium junceum (Spanish broom)

Symphoricarpos orbiculatus (St Peter's wort)

Syringa laciniata & *S. × persica*

Taxodium distichum (American deciduous or swamp cypress)

A NEW WORLD FLOWER GARDEN 1760 –1800

Roses
bracteata
'Burgundiaca'
'Celsiana'
× damascena semperflorens
'De Meaux'
'Enfant de France'
foetida 'Bicolor'
'Great Maiden's Blush'
hemisphaerica
moschata
'Noisette Carnée' (syn. 'Blush Noisette')
× odorata 'Pallida' (Old Blush China)
'Portlandica'
'Shailer's White Moss'
'Tuscany'
'Unique Blanche'

Flowers
Amaranthus hybridus var. *erythrostachys* (prince's feather)
Anoda cristata

Aster cordifolius, A. ericoides & *A. tradescantii*
Cassia marilandica
Chelone obliqua
Cimicifuga racemosa
Coreopsis verticillata
Cosmos bipinnatus
Dahlia coccinea & *D. pinnata*
Dicentra formosa
Dodecatheon meadia
Helianthus decapetalus double & *H. giganteus*
Ipomoea hederacea, I. purpurea & *I. quamoclit*
Lilium canadense, L. catesbaei & *L. superbum*
Nicandra physaloides
Penstemon campanulatus
Rudbeckia fulgida, R. hirta & *R. laciniata*
Sanvitalia procumbens
Silene dioica 'Rosea Plena'
Zinnia peruviana red form

A REGENCY FLOWER GARDEN 1800 –1840

Flowers
Alyssum saxatile
Anemone nemorosa double & coloured forms
Aster amellus
Aubrieta deltoidea
Campanula alliariifolia, C. carpatica & *C. lactiflora*
Chelidonium majus 'Plenum' (double greater celandine)
Chrysanthemum coronarium (white chrysanthemum)
Convallaria majalis double & pink lily-of-the-valley
Delphinium elatum
Dianthus sylvestris
Doronicum spp.
Gaillardia aristata
Geranium tuberosum
Hieracium aurantiacum & *H. pilosella*
Lathyrus vernus
Malva sylvestris mauritiana, M. verticillata & *M.v.* 'Crispa'
Papaver alpinum & *P. nudicaule*

Polemonium caeruleum
Primula vulgaris 'Alba Plena'
Pseudofumaria (Corydalis) lutea
Pulmonaria saccharata
Salvia nemorosa & *S. sylvestris*
Saxifraga × urbium (London pride)
Scilla siberica
Senecio elegans

Trees and Shrubs
Buddleja globosa
Buxus sempervirens cvs. ('Angustifolia', 'Argenteovariegata', 'Aureovariegata', 'Latifolia Maculata', 'Myrtifolia', 'Notata' & 'Suffruticosa Variegata')
Caragana arborescens
Ceanothus coeruleus
Cedrus deodara
Chaenomeles speciosa
Cornus florida
Crataegus crus-galli, C. laevigata 'Rosea Flore Pleno & *C. persimilis* 'Prunifolia'
Erica arborea
Gleditsia triacanthos
Halesia tetraptera
Hamamelis virginiana
Hypericum calycinum (rose of Sharon) *Ilex aquifolium* cvs. ('Argentea Marginata', 'Aurea Marginata', 'Bacciflava' & 'Ferox')
Jasminum fruticans
Kerria japonica
Ligustrum lucidum
Liriodendron tulipifera (tulip tree)
Magnolia denudata
Mahonia repens
Paeonia suffruticosa
Pinus cembra & *P. mugo*,
Prunus mahaleb, P. padus & *P. serrulata*
Pyrus salicifolia
Quercus × hispanica 'Fulhamensis' & *Q. × h.* 'Lucombeana'
Rhododendron arboreum, R. dauricum, R.calendulaceum, R. indicum, R. luteum, R. maximum, R. periclymenoides, R ponticum & *R. viscosum*
Ribes sanguineum

Rosa spp. & cvs. ('Agathe Incarnata', *banksiae* var. *banksiae* & *b.* 'Lutea', *bracteata, × centifolia* 'Bullata', *glauca*, 'Gloire de France', 'Ipsilanté', 'Leda', 'Marie *multiflora* 'Carnea' & *m.* 'Grevillei', *× odorata* 'Odorata' (Hume's Blush) & *× o.* 'Sanguinea', 'Rose d'Amour', 'Rose Edouard' & 'Spong')
Sophora japonica
Weigela florida

A NINETEENTH-CENTURY GARDEN OF THE DEEP SOUTH 1820 –1890

Flowers
Asclepias tuberosa
Baptisia australis
Browallia americana
Calceolaria pinnata
Cleome hassleriana
Datura metel
Dendranthema indicum (*Chrysanthemum i.*)
Dimorphotheca pluvialis (small Cape marigold)
Dorotheanthus bellidiformis (mesembryanthemum)
Eupatorium coelestinum
Hedyotis caerulea (*Houstonia c.*)
Hibiscus militaris (soldier rose mallow)
Lablab purpureus (*Dolichos lablab*)
Liatris pycnostachya, L . spicata & *L. squarrosa*
Mirabilis longiflora
Proboscidea louisianica (*Martynia l.*)

Foliage Plants
Euphorbia marginata
Fatsia japonica
Melianthus major
Nandina domestica
Ricinus communis
Yucca aloifolia, Y. filamentosa, Y. flaccida, Y. glauca & *Y. recurvifolia*

Kitchen Garden – Vegetables & Herbs

Brussels sprouts
common thyme
cornsalad (*Valerianella locusta*)
egg plant (aubergine)
fenugreek (*Trigonella foenum-graecum*)
groundnut (*Arachis hypogaea*)
horehound (*Marrubium vulgare*)
Mexican tea or wormseed (*Chenopodium ambrosioides*)
pinkroot (*Spigelia marilandica*)
potatoes
pot marjoram (*Origanum onites*)
Summer savory (*Satureja hortensis*) & winter s. (*S. montana*)
tomatoes
Virginia snake-root (*Aristolochia serpentaria*)

A MID-VICTORIAN ROSE GARDEN 1850 –1880

Shrub & Bush Roses

'Agatha'	Gallica
'Alain Blanchard'	Gallica
'A Longs Pédoncules'	Moss
'Assemblage des Beautés'	Gallica
'Baron de Wassenaer'	Moss
'Belle de Crécy'	Gallica
'Belle Isis'	Gallica
'Blanche de Vibert'	Portland
'Blanchefleur'	Centifolia
'Bon Silène'	Tea
'Bourbon Queen'	Bourbon
'Camaieux'	Gallica
'Céleste'	Alba
'Célina'	Moss
x *centifolia* 'Variegata'	
'Charles de Mills'	Gallica
'Chloris'	Alba
'Comtesse de Murinais'	Moss
'Cosimo Ridolfi'	Gallica
'Coupe d'Hébé'	Bourbon
'Cramoisi Picoté'	Gallica
'Cramoisi Supérieur'	China
'Duc de Guiche'	Gallica
'Duchesse d'Angoulême'	Gallica
'Duchesse de Montebello'	Gallica
'Du Maître d'Ecole'	Gallica
'Fabvier'	China
'Félicité Parmentier'	Alba

'Général Kléber'	Moss
'Georges Vibert'	Gallica
'Gloire des Mousseuses'	Moss
'Great Western'	Bourbon
x *harisonii* 'Harison's Yellow'	
'Henri Martin'	Moss
'Hermosa'	China
'Ispahan'	Damask
'James Veitch'	Moss
'Juno'	Centifolia
'Königin von Dänemark'	Alba
'Lanei'	Moss
'La Reine'	HP
'Le Vésuve'	China
'Louise Odier'	Bourbon
'Louis XIV'	China
'Mme Bravy'	Tea
'Mme Delaroche-Lambert'	Portland
'Mme Hardy'	Damask
'Mme Zoëtmans'	Damask
'Manning's Blush'	Hybrid Sweet Briar
'Malton'	Bourbon
'Marbrée'	Portland
'Mousseline'	Moss
'Nestor'	Gallica
x *odorata* 'Ochroleuca'	China
'Oeillet Parfait'	Gallica
'Ohl'	Gallica
'Ombrée Parfaite'	Gallica
'Pélisson'	Moss
'Petite Lisette'	Centifolia
'Prince Camille de Rohan'	HP
'Reine des Violettes'	HP
'René d'Anjou'	Moss
'Safrano'	Tea
'Salet'	Moss
'Souvenir de la Malmaison'	Bourbon
'Stanwell Perpetual'	Hybrid Scotch Briar
'Surpasse Tout'	Gallica
'Tour de Malakoff'	Gallica
'Tricolore de Flandre'	Gallica
'Violacea'	Gallica
'William Lobb'	Moss

Climbing & Rambling Roses

'Adam'	Cl Tea
'Adélaïde d'Orléans'	Rambler
'Amadis'	Boursault
'Baltimore Belle'	Rambler
'Blairii No 2'	Bourbon

'Blush Boursault'	Boursault
'Céline Forestier'	Noisette
'Champneys' Pink Cluster'	China x
'Cloth of Gold'	Noisette
'Devoniensis'	Cl Tea
'Flora'	Rambler
x *odorata* 'Fortune's Double Yellow'	China
'Gloire de Dijon'	Cl Tea
'Lamarque'	Noisette
'Mme D'Arblay'	Rambler
'Pompon de Paris, Climbing'	China
'Princesse de Nassau'	Rambler
'Princesse Marie'	Rambler
'Ruga'	Rambler
'Russelliana'	Rambler
'Sombreuil, Climbing'	Cl Tea
'Spectabilis'	Rambler
'Splendens'	Rambler
'The Garland'	Rambler

A VICTORIAN BACK GARDEN 1860 –1890

Wall Plants

Actinidia kolomikta
Akebia quinata
Clematis spp. & cvs. (pre 1880) ('Ascotiensis', 'Countess of Lovelace', 'Duchess of Edinburgh', 'Fair Rosamond', *florida* 'Flore Pleno' & *f.* 'Sieboldii', 'Henryi', 'Jackmanii Alba', 'Jackmanii Superba', 'Lady Londesborough', 'Mme Grangé', 'Miss Bateman', *montana*, 'Star of India', 'The President' & x *triternata*, 'Victoria')
Hedera helix 'Caenwoodiana', 'Cavendishii', 'Minor Marmorata', 'Palmata', *rhombea* 'Variegata'
Hydrangea anomala ssp. *petiolaris*
Jasminum officinale 'Argenteovariegatum'
Lonicera x *brownii, etrusca* & *japonica*
Parthenocissus tricuspidata (Boston ivy)

Solanum crispum
Trachelospermum jasminoides
Wisteria floribunda, W. f. macrobotrys & *W. sinensis*

Ferns

Adiantum capillus-veneris
Asplenium adiantum-niarum, A trichomanes cristatum & *A. t. incisum*
Athyrium filix-femina cristatum, A. f.-f. 'Minutissimum' & *A. f.-f.* 'Victoriae'
Blechnum spicant & *B. tabulare*
Cryptogramma crispa
Dryopteris affinis 'Cristata The King', *D. dilatata* 'Grandiceps' & *D. filix-mas* 'Grandiceps'
Osmunda regalis cristata
Phyllitis scolopendrium crispa
Polypodium vulgare 'Cornubiense'
Polystichum setiferum plumoso- divisilobum & *P. s. pulcherrimum*

Rhododendrons (pre 1880)

'Boddaertianum'
'Broughtonii'
'Caractacus'
'Caucasicum Pictum'
'Chevalier Felix de Sauvage'
'Cunningham's White'
'Edmondii'
'Everestianum'
'Fastuosum Flore Pleno'
'Isabella Mangles'
'Lady Eleanor Cathcart'
'Lee's Dark Purple'
'Mrs R.S. Holford'
'Nobleanum Coccineum'
'Nobleanum Venustum'
'Praecox'
'Prince Camille de Rohan'
'Roseum Elegans'

A VICTORIAN FLOWER GARDEN 1870–1900

Permanent bedding (can be left in situ through winter) marked *; winter/spring bedding marked +; remainder are summer bedding.

Dots

* *Abies balsamea* 'Hudsonia'
Abutilon cvs.
Agave attenuata
Araucaria araucana (young plants)
Artemisia arborescens
* *Aucuba japonica* 'Picturata' & *A. j.* 'Variegata'
* *Buxus sempervirens* cvs. ('Argenteovariegata', 'Aureovariegata', 'Elegantissima' & 'Latifolia Maculata') (clipped)
Canna × generalis
Centaurea cineraria spp. *cineraria* (*C. gymnocarpa*)
* *Chamaecyparis lawsoniana* 'Nana', *C. obtusa* 'Nana', *C. obtusa* 'Pygmaea' & *C. pisifera* 'Pygmaea'
Cordyline australis
Ensete ventricosum (*Musa ensete*)
Eucalyptus spp. (seedlings)
* *Euonymus japonicus* 'Ovatus Aureus' (pruned to shape)
Fuchsia (standards/pyramids)
Grevillea robusta
* *Ilex × altaclerensis* 'Golden King' & *I. × a.* 'Lawsoniana' (clipped)
* *Ilex aquifolium* cvs. (clipped)
* *Juniperus communis* 'Hibernica'
* *Picea abies* 'Gregoryana'
* *Skimmia japonica*
Sequoiadendron giganteum (young plants)

Grounds

Antirrhinum (single colours)
Begonia semperflorens
Calceolaria e.g. *C.* 'Camden Hero', *C. integrifolia* & *C.* 'Kentish Hero'
+ *Cheiranthus* (wallflower, single colours)

Dahlia bedding cvs.
+ *Myosotis* (forget-me-not)
+ Ornamental cabbage or kale
Pelargonium cvs. ('Flower of Spring', 'Dolly Vardon', 'Golden Harry Hieover', 'Henry Jacoby', 'King of Denmark', 'Mrs Pollock' & 'Red Black Vesuvius')
+ *Primula* (primrose & polyanthus, not large flowered cvs. in modern colours (blue, purple, pink))
+ *Viola* (winter pansies)

Underplanting

+ hyacinth cvs. ('Bismarck', 'Distinction', 'General Köhler', 'King of the Blues', 'Lady Derby', 'La Victoire', 'L'Innocence', 'Lord Balfour', 'Marie' & 'Oranje Boven')
+ *Muscari armeniacum*, *M. aucheri* & *M. azureum*
+ tulip cvs. ('Clara Butt', 'Couleur Cardinal', 'Greuze', 'Murillo', 'Peach Blossom', 'Pink Beauty', 'Prince of Austria' & 'Van der Neer')

Edgings

Ageratum houstonianum
+ *Alyssum saxatile* 'Compactum'
+ *Arabis caucasica*
+ *Aubrieta*
Begonia semperflorens
+ *Bellis perennis* cvs.
Calocephalus brownii
Centaurea rutifolia
Chlorophytum comosum (*C. elatum*)
Echeveria glauca
* *Euonymus japonicus* 'Microphyllus' (clipped)
* *Ilex crenata* (clipped)
Lobelia erinus
Pelargonium 'Mme Saileron'
* *Sempervivum* cvs.
Senecio bicolor spp. *cineraria*
Tanacetum 'Golden Feather'

A TRADITIONAL SCOTTISH POTAGER 1880–1910

Vegetables (pre 1900)

Seed of most of the varieties listed below is available from the Henry Doubleday Research Association, National Centre for Organic Gardening, Ryton-on-Dunsmore, Coventry CV8 3LG, England. The Association also produces *The Good Potato Guide* which gives descriptions and sources for the potatoes listed here.

asparagus 'Connover's Colossal'
bean, broad, 'Bunyard's Exhibition', 'Green Windsor', 'Johnson's Wonderful', 'Masterpiece' & 'White Windsor'
bean, dwarf French, 'Canadian Wonder' & 'Mont d'Or Golden Butter'
bean, runner, 'Painted Lady'
beetroot 'Detroit Globe' & 'Egyptian Turnip-Rooted'
broccoli 'Early Purple Sprouting'
cabbage (for autumn/winter eating) 'Red Drumhead' & 'Winnigstadt'
cabbage (for spring eating) 'Ellam's Early', 'Harbinger', 'Offenham' & 'Wheeler's Imperial'
cabbage, Savoy 'Ormskirk Extra Late' carrot 'Early Horn', 'Early Nantes', 'James's Scarlet Intermediate', 'Long Red Surrey' & 'St Valery'
cauliflower 'Purple Cape'
celery 'Clayworth Pink Prize'
chicory 'Brussels Witloof'
chicory (radicchio) 'Rosso di Treviso'
endive 'Batavian Green'
kale or borecole 'Dwarf Green Curled' & 'Tall Green Curled'
leek 'Monstruoso di Carantan', 'Musselburgh' & 'The Lyon'
lettuce, cabbage, 'All the Year Round', 'Favourite' & 'Tom Thumb'
lettuce, Cos, 'Balloon', 'Paris White' & 'Vaux's Self-Folding'
melon, Canteloupe, 'Blenheim Orange'

onion 'Ailsa Craig', 'Bedfordshire Champion', 'James's Long Keeping' & 'White Spanish'
parsley 'Champion Moss Curled'
parsnip 'Hollow Crown', 'Tender True' & 'The Student'
pea 'Alderman', 'Daisy', Early Onward', 'Gradus' & 'Thomas Laxton'
potato 'British Queen', 'Duke of York', 'Edzell Blue', 'Epicure', 'Pink Fir Apple', 'Royal Kidney' & 'Up-to-date'
radish, summer, 'Scarlet Globe'
radish, winter, 'China Rose', 'Long Black Spanish' & 'Round Black Spanish'
rhubarb 'Hawke's Champagne', 'Collis's Ruby', 'Daw's Champion', 'Early Albert', 'Linnaeus', 'Mitchell's Royal Albert', 'Prince Albert' & 'Victoria'
spinach 'Victoria'
turnip 'Green Top Stone', 'Snowball' & 'Veitch's Red Globe'

THE REVIVAL OF THE FORMAL GARDEN 1890–1920

Herbaceous Borders

Plants in cultivation by 1920

Achillea filipendulina 'Parker's Variety', *A. ptarmica* 'Perry's Variety' & *A. p.* 'Boule de Neige'
Aconitum × cammarum var. *bicolor* & *A. carmichaelii* var. *wilsonii*
Agapanthus campanulatus
Anemone × hybrida 'Géante des Blanches' & *A. hupehensis* var. *japonica* 'Prinz Heinrich'
Anthemis tinctoria 'E.C. Buxton' & *A. t.* 'Kelwayi'
Aquilegia Mrs Scott-Elliott's Hybrids
Artemisia lactiflora & *A. stelleriana*

Aster amellus 'King George',
  A. ericoides 'Hon. Edith Gibbs',
  A. 'Photograph', *A. novi-belgii*
  cvs. ('Anita Ballard', 'Climax',
  'Cloudy Blue', 'King of the
  Belgians', 'Perry's White', 'St
  Egwyn' & 'Snowdrift')
Astilbe cvs. ('Europa', 'Gloria',
  'Professor van der Wielen',
  'Queen Alexandra' & 'Venus')
Bergenia cordifolia, B. crassifolia
  & *B. × schmidtii*
Campanula 'Burghaltii',
  C. glomerata var. *dahurica* &
  C. persicifolia 'Telham Beauty'
Crocosmia cvs. ('Carmin Brillant',
  'Eldorado', 'George Davison',
  'Lady Hamilton', 'Queen
  Alexandra', 'Queen of Spain',
  'Solfaterre' & 'Star of the East')
Delphinium Belladonna cvs.
  ('Cliveden Beauty', 'Lamartine'
  & 'Moerheimii'
Dianthus cvs. ('Excelsior',
  'Inchmery', 'Mrs Sinkins' &
  'White Ladies')
Echinops ritro
Erigeron cvs. ('B. Ladhams' &
  'Quakeress')
Eryngium alpinum, E. ×
  oliverianum & *E. giganteum*
Euphorbia characias spp. *wulfenii*
Filipendula rubra 'Venusta'
Geranium × riversleaianum
  'Russell Prichard'
Geum 'Lady Stratheden'
Hosta fortunei 'Albomarginata' &
  H. sieboldiana elegans
Iris, Bearded cvs. ('Ambassadeur',
  'Bride', 'Honorabile', 'Hugh
  Miller' & 'Zua')
Kniphofia caulescens, K.
  'Goldelse', *K. northiae, K.* 'Star
  of Baden-Baden' & *K. uvaria*
  'Nobilis'
Leucanthemum × superbum (syn.
  Chrysanthemum maximum)
  'Marion Collier' & 'Mayfield
  Giant'
Monarda 'Cambridge Scarlet'

Paeonia lactiflora cvs. ('Albert
  Crousse', 'Baroness Schröder',
  'François Ortegat', 'Lady
  Alexandra Duff', 'Le Cygne',
  'Marie Crousse', 'Mme Jules
  Dessert', 'Mistral', 'M. Jules Elie',
  'M. Martin Cahuzac', 'Sarah
  Bernhardt' & 'Solange')
Papaver orientale cvs. ('Beauty of
  Livermere', 'Black and White',
  'King George', 'Mrs George
  Stobart', 'Mrs Perry', 'Perry's
  White' & 'Prinzessin Victoria
  Louise')
Penstemon cvs. ('George Home',
  'Myddelton Gem', 'Newbury
  Gem', 'Rubicundus' &
  'Southgate Gem')
Phlox paniculata cvs. ('Annie
  Laurie', 'Europe', 'Le Mahdi',
  'Rijnstroom' & 'The King')
Potentilla 'Gibson's Scarlet'
Salvia nemorosa & *S. sclarea*
Sedum spectabile & *S. telephium*
Sidalcea candida, S. malviflora &
  S. 'Rose Queen'
Stachys macrantha 'Robusta'
Thalictrum delavayi & *T.d. album*
Verbascum chaixii & *V.* 'Vernale'
Veronica exaltata

A TRADITIONAL COTTAGE
GARDEN 1880–1920

Anchusa azurea 'Dropmore' &
  A.i. 'Opal'
Anemone × hybrida 'Alba',
  'Elegans', 'Honorine Jobert',
  'Königin Charlotte', 'Monterosa'
  & 'Whirlwind'
Astilbe × arendsii 'Ceres', *A. × a.*
  'Rosa Perle', *A. × rosea* 'Peach
  Blossom' & *A. × r.* 'Queen
  Alexandra'
Crocosmia × crocosmiiflora
  (montbretia)
Dendranthema (chrysanthemum)
  rubellum 'Anastasia' &
  'Emperor of China'
Galega × hartlandii
Geranium × endressii & *G. ×*
  magnificum
Geum 'Borisii' & 'Mrs J. Bradshaw'

Helenium 'Riverton Beauty'
Helianthus 'Soleil d'Or'
Hemerocallis 'Baroni'
Iris germanica 'Kochii'
Paeonia lactiflora cvs. ('Couronne
  d'Or', 'Duchesse de Nemours',
  'Edulis Superba', 'Félix
  Crousse', 'Festiva Maxima',
  'François Ortegat', 'Mme Calot',
  'Mme Lemoine', 'Marie
  Lemoine', 'Philomèle' & 'Reine
  Hortense')
Phlox paniculata cvs. ('Eclaireur',
  'Elizabeth Campbell', 'Frau
  Antoine Buchner' & 'The King')
Tanacetum (*Pyrethrum*)
  coccineum 'James Kelway'
Scabiosa caucasica & *S. c. alba*
Solidago 'Golden Wings'
Veronica gentianoides &
  V. g. 'Variegata'

A JEKYLLESQUE GARDEN
1890–1930

Roses in cultivation by 1902, from
Roses for English Gardens by G.
Jekyll & E. Mawley

Bush and Shrub Roses

'Alfred Colomb'	HP
'Anna Olivier'	Tea
'Anne of Geierstein'	Hybrid Sweet Briar
'Antoine Rivoire'	HT
'Augustine Guinoisseau'	HT
'Baroness Adolph de Rothschild'	HP
'Beauty of Waltham'	HP
'Captain Hayward'	HP
'Catherine Mermet'	Tea
'Cécile Brunner'	Polyantha
'Charles Lefèbvre'	HP
'Cramoisi Supérieur'	China
'Dr Andry'	HP
'Dr Grill'	Tea
'Duke of Edinburgh'	HP
'Fellenberg'	China
'Fisher and Holmes'	HP
'Général Jacqueminot'	HP
'Gloire Lyonnaise'	HP
'Gruss an Teplitz'	China
'Her Majesty'	HP

'Homère'	Tea
'Horace Vernet'	HP
'Janet's Pride'	Hybrid Sweet Briar
'Lady Penzance'	Hybrid Sweet Briar
'La France'	HT
'Mme Caroline Testout'	HT
'Mme de Watteville'	Tea
'Mme Eugène Résal'	Tea
'Mme Gabriel Luizet'	HP
'Mme Laurette Messimy'	China
'Marchioness of Salisbury'	HT
'Marie van Houtte'	Tea
'Meg Merrilies'	Hybrid Sweet Briar
'Mrs John Laing'	HP
'Perle d'Or'	Polyantha
'Prince Camille de Rohan'	HP
'Souvenir d'Elise Vardon'	Tea
'Souvenir de la Malmaison'	Bourbon
'Souvenir du Président Carnot'	HT
'Stanwell Perpetual'	Hybrid Scotch Briar
'The Bride'	Tea
'Ulrich Brunner Fils'	HP
'White Pet'	Polyantha

Climbing & Rambler Roses

'Aimée Vibert'	Noisette
'Alister Stella Gray'	Noisette
'Anemone'	
'Bennett's Seedling'	Rambler
'Bouquet d'Or'	Noisette
'Claire Jacquier'	Noisette
'Mme Alfred Carrière'	Noisette
'Maréchal Niel'	Noisette
'Reine Marie Henriette'	HT/Climber
'The Garland'	Rambler
'William Allen Richardson'	Noisette

A POST-WAR SUBURBAN GARDEN 1920–1940

Shrub Border

Abelia × *grandiflora*
Acer japonicum &
    A. palmatum cvs .
Berberis buxifolia, B candidula,
    B. darwinii, B. gagnepainii var
    . *lanceifolia, B.* × *stenophylla* &
    B. thunbergii atropurpurea
Buddleja davidii
Ceanothus × *delileanus* 'Gloire de
    Versailles'
Ceratostigma willmottianum
Choisya ternata
Cornus alba 'Elegantissima' &
    C. a. 'Spaethii'
Cotoneaster adpressus, C. bullatus,
    C. dammeri var. *radicans,*
    C. franchetii, C. horizontalis &
    C. salicifolius
Cytisus x *beanii, C.* × *kewensis* &
    C. scoparius 'Andreanus'
Daphne cneorum
Deutzia × *elegantissima,*
    D. gracilis, D. × *kalmiiflora,*
    D. longifolia 'Veitchii', *D.* ×
    magnifica, D. × *rosea* &
    D. scabra 'Plena'
Elaeagnus angustifolia,
    E. commutata, E. pungens
    'Aurea', *E. p.* 'Frederici',
    E. p. 'Maculata' &
    E. p. 'Variegata'
Escallonia 'Donard Seedling',
    E. 'Edinensis', *E.* 'Ingramii',
    E . × *langleyensis* & *E. rubra*
Euonymus alatus, E. japonicus
    'Albomarginatus', *E. j.* 'Aureus',
    E.j. 'Latifolius
    Albomarginatus' &
    E. j. 'Ovatus Aureus'
Exochorda × *macrantha*
Forsythia × *intermedia* 'Spectabilis',
    F. ovata & *F. suspensa*
    atrocaulis
Fuchsia magellanica var. *gracilis*
    'Variegata'
Genista aetnensis
Hebe × *andersonii, H. anomala,*
    H. cupressoides & *H.* ×
    franciscana 'Blue Gem'

Hibiscus syriacus 'Coelestis',
    H. s. 'Hamabo' &
    H. s 'Snowdrift'
Hydrangea arborescens
    'Grandiflora', *H. a.* spp.
    discolor 'Sterilis',
    H. macrophylla cvs. &
    H. serrata
Ilex × *altaclerensis* cvs.
Kerria japonica 'Picta'
Magnolia stellata
Mahonia japonica & *M. j. bealei*
Osmanthus delavayi
Perovskia atriplicifolia
Philadelphus cvs. ('Boule d'Argent',
    'Bouquet Blanc', 'Burfordensis',
    'Coupe d'Argent', 'Erectus' &
    'Virginal')
Pieris formosa var. *forrestii* &
    P. japonica
Ribes sanguineum 'Brocklebankii'
    & *R. s.* 'King Edward VII'
Sambucus racemosa 'Plumosa
    Aurea'
Skimmia japonica 'Rubella', *S. j.*
    'Veitchii' & *S. j. reevesiana*
Sorbaria aitchisonii
Spiraea 'Arguta' & *S. japonica*
    'Anthony Waterer'
Syringa vulgaris cvs. ('Andenken
    an Ludwig Späth', 'Belle de
    Nancy', 'Charles Joly',
    'Condorcet', 'Congo', 'Mme
    Antoine Buchner', 'Mme
    Lemoine', 'Michel Buchner',
    'Paul Thirion', 'Président Grévy'
    & 'Vestale')
Viburnum carlesii, V. davidii,
    V. farreri, V. plicatum 'Mariesii'
    & *V. p.* 'Sterile'
Weigela 'Abel Carrière', *W.* 'Eva
    Rathke' & *W. florida*

A POST-WAR SUNKEN GARDEN 1920–1940

Emergent Plants

Acorus calamus 'Variegatus' &
    A. gramineus 'Variegatus'
Butomus umbellatus
Calla palustris (bog arum)
Carex elata 'Aurea' (Bowles'
    golden sedge)

Cyperus involucratus
    (tender – overwinter indoors)
Glyceria maxima ' Variegata'
Iris ensata, I. laevigata 'Alba',
    I. l. 'Colchesterensis', *I. l.*
    'Variegata', *I. pseudacorus,*
    I. p. 'Variegata' & *I.* 'Rose
    Queen'
Lysichiton americanus &
    L. camtschatcensis
Narthecium ossifragum (bog
    asphodel)
Orontium aquaticum (golden
    club)
Sagittaria sagittifolia 'Flore Pleno'
Saururus cernuus
Scirpus lacustris 'Albescens' &
    S. l. spp. *tabernaemontani*
    'Zebrinus'
Typha angustifolia, T. laxmannii
    & *T. minima*
Zantedeschia aethiopica &
    Z. a. 'Little Gem'

Waterlilies

(Nymphaea spp. & cvs. *)*
The following hardy varieties raised
or introduced before 1920 may be
grown in as little as l ft/30 cm of
water.

'Albatros'
'Atropurpurea'
'Attraction'
'Aurora'
candida
'Comanche'
'Ellisiana'
'Graziella'
× *helvola*
'Hermine'
'Laydekeri Fulgens'
'Laydekeri Lilacea'
'Laydekeri Purpurata'
'Laydekeri Rosea'
'Odorata Minor'
'Pygmaea Rubis'
'Rosennymphe'
'Sioux'
'Solfatare'
tetragona

FURTHER READING

There is an ever increasing literature on garden history, the majority of it produced over the last ten to fifteen years. Readers should be warned that very few of the books listed below deal with the reality of hands-on period gardening.
*Those books marked with an * contain period plant lists*

General Histories

Adams, William Howard, *The French Garden 1500-1800*, Scholar Press, London, 1979
Bazin, Germain, *Paradeisos, The Art of the Garden*, Cassell, London, 1990
Berrall, Julia, *The Garden, An Illustrated History*, Viking, 1966
Duthie, Ruth, *Florists' Flowers and Societies*, Shire Publications, 1988
Halliwell, Brian, *Old Flower Gardens*, Bishopsgate Press, 1987
Harvey, John, *Early Gardening Catalogues*, Phillimore, Chichester, 1972
Harvey, John, *Early Nurserymen*, Phillimore, Chichester, 1974
Masson, Georgina, *Italian Gardens*, Antique Collectors Club, Woodbridge, Suffolk, 1961
Mosser, Monique and Teyssot, Georges, *The History of Garden Design, The Western Tradition from the Renaissance to the Present Day*, Thames & Hudson, London, 1991
Taylor, M. and Hill, C. *Hardy Plants Introduced to Britain by 1799*, 2nd edition revised, Cranborne Garden Centre, 1983

Ages of Adventure

* Harvey, John, *Medieval Gardens*, Batsford, London, 1961
* Lazzaro, Claudia, *The Italian Renaissance Garden*, Yale University Press, New Haven and London, 1990
McClean, Teresa, *Medieval English Gardens*, Collins, London, 1981
Shepherd, J.C., and Jellicoe, G.A., *Italian Gardens of the Renaissance 1925* reissued by Academy editions, London, 1986
Strong, Roy, *The Renaissance Garden in England*, Thames & Hudson, London, 1979

Age of Display

The Anglo-Dutch Garden in the Age of William and Mary, Journal of Garden History, VIII, nos 2 and 3, 1988
* Jacques, David, and Horst, *Arend Jan van der, The Gardens of William and Mary*, Christopher Helm, London, 1988
* Leighton, Ann, *Early American Garden, "For Meate of Medicine"*, University of Massachussetts Press, 1970
Williams, Dorothy Hunt, *Historic Gardens of Virginia*, The Garden Club of Virginia, 1975
* Woodbridge, Kenneth, *Princely Gardens, The origins and development of the French formal style*, Thames & Hudson, London, 1956

Age of Elegance

Crulckshank, Dan, and Burton, Neil, *Life in the Georgian City*, Viking, Penguin, 1990
Jacques, David, Georgian Gardens, *The Reign of Nature*, Batsford, London, 1953
* Leighton, Ann, *American Gardens of the Eighteenth Century, "For Use or Delight"*, University of Massachussetts Press, 1976
Martin, Peter, *The Pleasure Gardens of Virginia*, Princeton University Press, 1991
Stuart, David C., *Georgian Gardens*, Batsford London, 1979

Age of Opulence

Carter, Tom, *The Victorian Garden*, Bell & Hyman, London, 1984
Clayton-Payne, Andrew, *Victorian Flower Gardens*, Weidenfeld & Nicolson, London, 1988
Elliott, Brent, *Victorian Gardens*, Batsford, London, 1986
Hobhouse, Penelope, and Wood, Christopher, *Painted Gardens, English Watercolours 1850–1914*, Pavilion Books, London, 1989
* Leighton, Ann, *American Gardens of the Nineteenth Century, "For Comfort and Affluence"*, University of Massachussetts Press, 1987

Age of Nostalgia

Brown, Jane, *The English Garden in our Time from Gertrude Jekyll to Geoffrey Jellicoe*, Antique Collector's Club, Woodbridge, Suffolk, 1986
Jekyll, Gertrude, and Weaver, Lawrence, *Gardens for Small Country Houses*, London, 1912 and several later editions
Ottewill, David, *The Edwardian Garden*, Yale University Press, New Haven and London, 1989 Seidenberg, Charlotte, *The New Orleans Garden*, Silkmont and Count, New Orleans, 1990

Re-creation and Restoration

*Banks, Elizabeth, *creating Period Gardens*, Phaidon, Oxford, 1991
* Pavretti, Rudy J., and Favretti, Joy Putnam, *Landscape and Gardens for Historic Buildings*, American Association for State and Local History, Nashville, 1979
Favretti, Rudy J., and Favretti, Joy Putnam, *For Every House a Garden*, University Press of New England, Hanover, New Hampshire, 1990
* Harvey, John, *Restoring Period Gardens*, Shire Garden History, 1988

Plants Lists

* Harvey, *Early Gardening Catalogues*, Phillimore, Chichester, 1972
* Harvey, John, *The Availability of Hardy Plants of the Late Eighteenth Century*, Garden History Society, 1988
* Stuart, David, and Sutherland, James, *Plants from the Past, Old Flowers for New Gardens*, Viking Penguin, London, 1987

INDEX

ACKNOWLEDGMENTS

The publisher thanks the following photographers and organizations for their kind permission to reproduce the photographs in this book:

2 W A Lord; 3 Bridgeman Art Library (City of Bristol Museum & Art Gallery); 6-7 Andrew Lawson; 8-9 Jerry Harpur (King Henry's Hunting Lodge); 10 John Miller; 11 above Jerry Pavia/Garden Picture Library; 11 below Jerry Harpur (designer Thomas Church); 12 Jerry Harpur (designer Michael Balston); 13 W A Lord; 14 Georges Lévêque; 15 Hugh Palmer; 16-19 Andrew Lawson; 20-21 Osterreichische Nationalbibliothek; 22 Andrew Lawson; 23 Derek Fell/Garden Picture Library; 24 Gary Rogers; 25 Alex Ramsay/Garden Picture Library; 26 above Nigel Temple/Garden Picture Library; 26 below Georges Lévêque; 27 Andrew Lawson; 28 Lamontagne; 29 Brigitte Thomas; 33 above left British Library Reproductions; 33 right Biblioteque Nationale, Paris; 33 below MAS/Capilla Real, Granada; 37 right Scala, Florence; 41 right Arbury Hall, Nuneaton (photographer John Wright); 41 below centre The Master and Fellows of Trinity College, Cambridge; 42-43 Yale Center for British Art (Paul Mellon Collection); 44 Eric Crichton (Hornbeam, Ham House); 45 Eric Crichton (Westbury Court); 46-47 Andrew Lawson; 48 Peter Baistow; 49 above Historic Annapolis Foundation; 49 below Gillian Darley/Edifice; 53 above left Musée de l'Ile de France à Sceaux (P Lemaitre); 53 above right British Library Reproductions; 53 below from *Den Nederlandtsen Hovenier* published by Stichting Matrys Utrecht; 57 above left Department Special Collections Library, Wagemingen Agricultural University (from *The Gardens of William & Mary* published by Christopher Helm/B. T. Batsford Ltd); 57 above right from *Den Nederlandtsen Hovenier* published by Stichting Matrys Utrecht; 57 below Amsterdams Historisch Museum; 61 above centre Colonial Williamsburg Foundation; 61 centre left Courtesy the Linley Library; 61 centre right British Library Reproductions; 61 below British Library Reproductions; 62-63 City of Bristol Museum & Art Gallery; 64 Heather Angel; 65 above Andrew Lawson; 65 below Derek Fell; 66-67 John Bethell; 68 Lamontagne; 69 above Andrew Lawson; 69 below Gillian Darley/Edifice; 73 above left Bodleian Library, Oxford; 73 below left Courtesy John Harris (Mrs Paul Mellon Collection); 77 above left National Trust, Southern Region (The Collection of Tom Parr); 77 below left British Library Reproductions; 77 below centre British Architectural Library, RIBA, London; 77 centre right Beinecke Rare Book and Manuscript Library, Yale University; 81 above right Devonshire Collection, Chatsworth. Reproduced by permission of the Chatsworth Settlement Trustees; 81 below Skipwith Papers, Swem Library, College of William & Mary; 81 above left from *The Historic Gardens of Virginia*, 1930; 85 above private collection; 85 centre from *The Florist's Manual* by Maria Jackson; 85 below British Library Reproductions; 86-87 Reproduced by kind permission of the Harris Museum & Art Gallery, Preston; 89 Hugh Palmer; 90 Andrew Lawson; 91 Hugh Palmer; 92-93 W A Lord; 94 Lamontagne; 95 Andrew Lawson; 99 New Orleans Botanical Archive; 103 above right Courtesy Christopher Wood Gallery; 103 below Apollo Publishers; 107 above left Mary Evans Picture Library; 107 below left Photo Museum of London (Courtesy Butters Family); 111 above Courtesy the Linley Library; 111 below from *The Amateur Flower Garden* by Shirley Hibberd; 115 above Bridgeman Art Library (By permission of the Trustees of the Royal Watercolour Society, Bankside Gallery, London); 115 centre right Apollo Publishers; 115 below centre Country Life; 115 below right from *Garden Planning* by W S Rogers published by Unwin; 116-117 By courtesy of the Medici Society Ltd, London and the artist's grandson; 118 Georges Lévêque (Parc Floral d'Apremont, La Guerche-Sur L'Aubois); 119 W A Lord; 120 Georges Lévêque; 121 above Georges Lévêque; 121 below Jerry Harpur (Hestercombe); 122 S & O Mathews; 123 W A Lord; 124 Eric Crichton (Hidcote); 125 Jerry Harpur (Tintinhull House); 129 above centre Country Life; 129 above right from Pigytle Works catalogue; 129 below centre from *The Formal Garden in England* by Reginald Blomfield; 129 below right Apollo Publishers; 133 above Courtesy Christopher Wood Gallery; 133 below Bridgeman Art Library (Courtesy Christopher Wood Gallery); 137 above Country Life; 137 below from *Modern Gardens* published by The Studio; 141 above Bridgeman Art Library (Bonhams); 141 below Country Life; 145 above from *Landscape Gardening* by Richard Sudell published by Ward Lock & Co; 145 below left from *Modern Gardens British and Foreign* published by The Studio; 145 below right from *Garden Design Annual* 1931.

Every effort has been made to trace the copyright holders and we apologize in advance for any unintentional omission and would be pleased to insert the appropriate acknowledgment in any subsequent edition of this publication.